ETHICAL WISDOM *for* FRIENDS

How to Navigate Life's Most Complicated, Curious, and Common Relationship Dilemmas

MARK MATOUSEK

Health Communications, Inc.
Deerfield Beach, Florida

www.hcibooks.com

Library of Congress Cataloging-in-Publication Data

Matousek, Mark.

Ethical wisdom for friends / Mark Matousek.
        p. cm.
    ISBN 978-0-7573-1727-9 (pbk.) — ISBN 0-7573-1727-8 (pbk.) — ISBN 978-
0-7573-1736-1 (ePub) — ISBN 0-7573-1736-7 (epub) 1. Friendship I. Title.
    BJ1533.F8M336 2013
    177'.62—dc23

                                                                                    2012032567

Publisher: Health Communications, Inc.
        3201 S.W. 15th Street
        Deerfield Beach, FL 33442-8190

Cover design by Larissa Hise Henoch
Interior design and formatting by Lawna Patterson Oldfield

Contents

I can sail without wind.
I can row without oars.
But I cannot part from my
friend without tears.

—S<small>WEDISH</small> F<small>OLK</small> S<small>ONG</small>

Acknowledgments

M y deepest thanks to the friends, students, and readers who were generous enough to tell me their stories. Also to my agent, Joy Harris, and to Allison Janse for editorial patience and expertise. Most of all, I'm grateful to David Moore who inspired me to write this book, and to whom it is dedicated.

Introduction

Recently, I opened my mailbox to find a letter from a concerned reader in Duluth, Minnesota. "Dear Sir: I just finished reading your book *Ethical Wisdom: The Search for a Moral Life* and wanted to send you a word of warning."

I steeled myself to be reprimanded for some factual error or political incorrectness, but this thirty-four-year-old attorney (and mother of two) had another agenda. "There's a saying in AA that understanding is the booby prize," she wrote.

"While I learned a lot from your book about what makes us moral, I knew zilch about how to put this stuff into practice. It's great to know that mirror neurons cause empathy—that blew my mind—but how does that help me make better choices? What difference does this knowledge make? If you ever write a book called 'Ethical Wisdom for Internet Dating,' or something like that, be sure to keep me on your list."

The lawyer from Minnesota was right. I had wanted to give lay readers like myself, a memoir writer by trade, an entertaining, un-PC map of how and why humans are hardwired for moral awareness, a bird's-eye view from a variety of sources: neuroscience, psychology, evolutionary biology, anthropology, philosophy, and behavioral economics. Thanks to breakthroughs with the fMRI machine, we are reaching a level of self-transparency beyond our wildest imaginings. We now understand that the brain is hardwired with a kind of moral organ—a matrix of faculties—that gear us toward ethical intelligence.

Researching the book, I learned things that permanently changed how I understood myself and the world. But I had not permitted myself to be prescriptive. I had not drawn conclusions or addressed specific groups of people with specific complications in their lives. Internet dating. Parents. Business. Office life. Lovers. My aerial view of the human condition had never quite put readers on the ground in any accessible, practical way. *Ethical Wisdom* was addressed at humans. But human beings were people, too, with complicated lives to sort out.

I've put together this collection of people stories from a variety of sources. Personal experience, student testimonials, interviews, and letters from readers provided a reservoir rich in wisdom about friendship, commitment, honesty, greed, jealousy, loyalty, competition, imitation, abandonment, and reconciliation. My hope is that these stories become good companions to you on your journey.

ONE

To Gossip Is Human

The most painful breakup of my life came when my four best friends dumped me, simultaneously, over an incident involving gossip. I meant no harm by my slip of the tongue to this mutual friend who, I assumed, knew this tidbit already. Still, I became persona non grata, the not-to-be-trusted, the blabbermouth, and, finally, the exile. They shut me out of their lives overnight, sending me into a year of therapy where I questioned my worth as a human being and someone to whom others might risk telling secrets.

The hardest part of this situation was the certainty that I meant no harm. The second-hardest part was knowing what gossip hounds each of these ex-friends was, too, and how much we'd enjoyed comparing notes, every single one of us, for years with one another. How had this suddenly become such a sin? In fact, it was the nature of the gossip—our mutual friend's infidelity—and the guilt she felt over it that had been sidetracked as blame onto me. But knowing this didn't give me my friends back.

"They shot the messenger," said my therapist. He explained that when guilt exists in a group, somebody's head's got to roll in order to ease the collective conscience. Consumed by the need for justice—accepted or not—I decided to try to understand gossip: what it is, where it comes from, and why human beings enjoy it so much. According to anthropologists, gossip has been integral to the survival of our species. In fact, human language developed specifically to enable us to gossip. Since the time of early man, our ancestors have used gossip as a social controlling device to keep each other in line. At first, language had evolved as a replacement for physical grooming. The leap from picking each others' lice to biting each others' backs seems to have come naturally to our nosy species. Since then, gossip has been an indispensable method for policing one another, helping us to monitor good and evil as well as prevent physical conflict. That's because gossip is our first line of defense before violence in the exertion of social control. Before we punch someone in the face, or torch his house, we can always ruin his reputation.

Humans use language primarily to talk *about* other people, to find out who's doing what, who's sleeping with so-and-so's husband, who cheated whom, who behaved heroically, or who caved in. By definition, gossip tends to be overwhelmingly critical, concerned primarily with moral and social violations. This is because individuals who were able to share information had an advantage in human evolution. Our ancestors surmised that, in a gossipy world, what we do matters less than what people think we do, so we'd better be able to frame our actions in a positive light.

"As ultrasocial creatures, we're also ultra-manipulators, fabricators, and competitors for the driver's seat," I wrote in *Ethical Wisdom*. Gossip created "a runaway competition in who could be master of the art of social manipulation, relationship aggression, and reputation management" in human society, as E. O. Wilson tells us. We also learned to prepare ourselves for other people's attempts to deceive, compete against, and manipulate *us*. A good reputation is social collateral, and gossip is key to how we protect it. As a moral controlling device, it allows us to save face and cast aspersions on others. We are not autonomously moral beings, after all. The more closely people live together, the more they care; the more they care, the more they gossip; and the more they gossip, the more language can serve its ethical function. "Gossip paired with reciprocity allows karma to work here on earth, not in the next life," psychologist Jonathan Haidt has quipped. In other words, gossip is natural, human, and indispensable. The important thing is to be aware of when, how, and with whom you gossip. Information is power, after all. We say things innocently that have a potential to wreck people's lives. Gossip should not be indulged in every time we feel like it any more than other natural functions are carried out indiscriminately. It means simply that gossip is natural, and that our urge to share personal information (particularly regarding those who matter to us most) has a long historic precedent and a positive social value when exercised skillfully. In the teachings of the Buddha, there are three helpful criteria for determining when to open our mouths. Before spilling the beans, or airing a grievance, Buddhism teaches us to ask ourselves these three questions in testing personal motivation. First, is the information *true*? Second, is sharing the information *necessary*? Finally, is the act of revelation *kind*? For friends, kindness is the bottom line; if information does not serve a caring function, we're wise to keep it to ourselves.

In fact, caring for my friend is what prompted this gossip. Disturbed by the infidelity, since we were equal friends with her boyfriend, I was sharing the unexpected news with a mutual friend in order to get a handle on it. I was not broadcasting it among strangers or bad-mouthing her in any way. During our estrangement, I would warn my friends in the sporadic grief notes I wrote for myself that they'd eventually come to see that they were wrong. This is exactly what came to pass. My four friends came to me, separately, asking me if I would forgive them. They were wrong to make me the scapegoat, they said, since it was the infidelity—not my gossip—that was the actual culprit (the couple had broken up by then). I felt both relieved and vindicated; I also do not trust them in quite the same way. I'm more careful about what I say to them. We feel much less close, less open, less like family. Maybe that's a good thing. Still, I miss it.

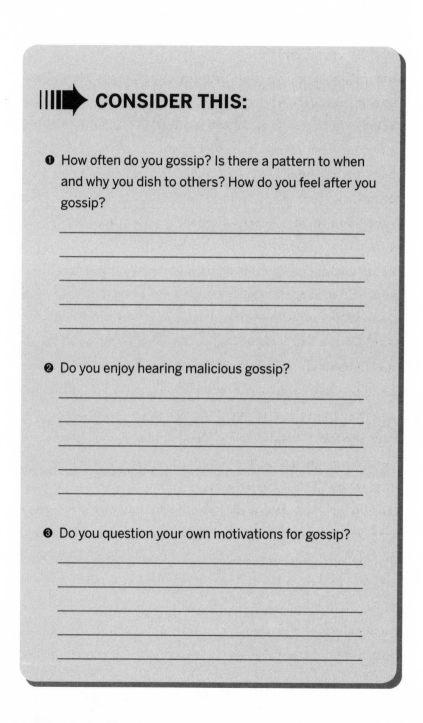

CONSIDER THIS:

❶ How often do you gossip? Is there a pattern to when and why you dish to others? How do you feel after you gossip?

_____

_____

_____

_____

_____

❷ Do you enjoy hearing malicious gossip?

_____

_____

_____

_____

❸ Do you question your own motivations for gossip?

_____

_____

_____

_____

_____

❹ Is it ever permissible to reveal a friend's secrets?
If so, when and why?

_____

_____

_____

_____

_____

❺ What is the relationship between loyalty and gossip?
Do you see yourself as your brother's keeper?
Why or why not?

_____

_____

_____

_____

_____

TWO

It's None of Your Business

Though gossip is inevitable, it also gives us a false sense of power. While evolution has prepared us to dish about others, it has not provided us with the power to change them in any way whatsoever, no matter how brilliant our advice might be. This can be excruciating. How can a normal, controlling person care intensely about his friends without trying to change them? How can we offer our treasured advice without being attached to its implementation? How can we watch in horror as our friends make the same terrible choices again and again—and again—without the urge to slap them? Shouldn't power be part of the friendship contract, a modicum of influence (read: control) to help guide the people we love so much in the effort to save them from themselves?

The answer is absolutely not. We're not meant to have any control whatsoever over how our friends behave. That is because it is none of our business. Our opinions about the lives of our friends are void of inherent importance or meaning. It's the price of loving individuals endowed with a measure of free will. Control is never, ever an option. No more can we influence the lives of our friends than they can steer our lives for us. This is the slipperiest slope on friendship mountain, the most demanding incline of all: How to be hands off and hands on at the same time; committed but not attached; attentive but not invasive; present yet distant. This distance is extremely important. Friendship requires both distance and closeness, like any intimacy, which is why knowing when to keep our mouths shut is such a virtue. A measure of detachment proves to our friends that we love them for who they are rather than who we want them to be, the self they could be if they were perfect (and listened to us).

Pam didn't know what to do about Tyler. None of us knew what to do about Tyler. A mutual friend for twenty-five years, Tyler counted both Pam and me as two of his shortest-list friends for life, and both of us were at our wits' end (Pam even more than me). The issue was sex, which Tyler was having to great excess and Pam believed should not be discussed, and certainly not on the Internet. With his fiftieth birthday approaching fast, our once dignified friend had grown increasingly vocal about his increasingly frequent hookups with women a whole lot younger than he was, crowing on a blog about his too-numerous conquests like Casanova on too much Cialis. Both of us were concerned for him. Actually, we were mortified. "What are we going to do?" Pam shrieked with puritanical horror. "No idea—" "Somebody's got to stop him!" she cried. "How?" "He's making a goddamn fool of himself." As Pam said this, I felt a pain in my conscience. Twenty years before, when Tyler and I were in our twenties, we had entered into a solemn vow to warn each other if either one was being age-inappropriate, or embarrassing himself in public. We made this promise to each other at a café in Paris one afternoon. A lecherous codger at the next table was putting the moves on a pretty coed, his Engelbert Humperdinck disco shirt unbuttoned below his hairy paunch. We watched with disgust as he pawed at the ingénue, who finally threw a ten-franc note at the table and stormed off. That's when Tyler turned to me with a serious look on his handsome face. "Never ever let me do that," he said. "Mutton dressed as lamb," I said. "I would rather be dead." We had vowed to watch each other's back. That's what friends were for, we agreed. But I never had cause to uphold this bargain till now. Pam insisted that I was the one to do it since I was Tyler's best male friend. Still, the prospect made me ill.

"The sooner, the better," she said gravely. I promised and hung up. Though Pam had a point, I was worried about interfering. Something about this didn't feel right. I felt as if I were trespassing, disrespecting Tyler, putting my nose where it didn't belong.

Part of the reason that we'd been best friends for thirty years is

that Tyler and I do not bust each other's chops. We are, constitutionally, very different people. Over the years, it has frequently
been necessary for me to suspend judgment and keep my mouth
shut. By warning him off his flaunted promiscuity, I would be
touching on deeper, more disturbing issues in Tyler's life, including his inability to commit, or satisfy himself with one person. In
my opinion, sexually speaking, Tyler was gorging at the smorgas-
bord and never getting a good square meal. But Tyler did not see
it that way, nor did he seem to feel poorly about it. Was Tyler's
promiscuity a smoke screen for loneliness? Yes. Was it my job to
make him feel bad about it? I wasn't sure.

Pondering how to help my friend, the words of a wise teacher
I once studied with came to mind. "There are only three kinds
of business in the world," she said. "My business. Your business.
And God's business." I knew that she was right. In the instant
my teacher said this, a lifetime of blurred relationship boundaries became clear. As a nosy, controlling, insecure person, these
words offered liberation from the presumptuous belief that I was
responsible for somebody else's choices. I was free not to pretend
to be able to change them; I was also free from trying to know
God's business, and make everything work out the way it should.
My business. Your business. And God's business. It was very hard
to argue with that.

Since then, I had remembered this motto whenever the urge to
meddle seized me. What my friends did was not my business. So
what should I do with Tyler, exactly? I knew what I wanted to say
to him: that the issue was privacy not sex. He could sleep with all

the ladies he chose but why make it a blogging event? Why publish things that he might regret—information that others were finding distasteful—in the virtual human mall where information lives forever? Could a little restraint or decorum hurt? That is all I wanted to ask him.

We met the following week for a powwow. Tyler was in fine form. The night before, he'd hooked up with a woman he met in the line at Duane Reade. "Ultra foxy. Twenty-nine. She told me I looked like Tony Bennett." "You don't look anything like Tony Bennett." "I know! She'd been drinking. My bad!" To make Tyler's midlife crisis worse, he was now abusing teen Twitter lingo. "She told me that I rocked the house." "The house is old," I couldn't help saying. Tyler ordered a Red Bull on the rocks. "I never understood sex before," he told me. "That's what's ironic. You know what I mean?" I shook my head. "It took me fifty years to figure it out. Women love me. They say I'm a catch. I used to think I was nothing special. Now, I know I'm filet mignon! Maybe I'll make that my next blog. 'From Chopped Liver to Filet Mignon.' What do you think? Too much? I don't want people to think I'm conceited." "I wondered about that. The conceited part. Maybe—" I chose my words carefully, "a little discretion might not hurt?" Tyler looked at me with pity. "I mean, it's not really anyone's business—" "You're right," he said. "No offense, dude—but you really need to loosen up. It's a new day. A new way of thinking. I've been meaning to tell you—" "Tell me what?" "Life doesn't have to be so goddamn serious." "I love my life." "I love mine, too," Tyler said. "This is the best time I've had in years. I feel free!

I don't give a shit what people think. Remember what a prig I used to be?" I nodded. "I look in the mirror now and think, *Watch out world! Big boy's in town.* I know what people are saying about me—" "You do?" "They think that I should act my age. They think that I'm an embarrassment. I should toe the line, button it up, play the dignified middle-aged man. Well, guess what? They can keep it. If people don't like what I'm doing, screw them. I mean that in all sincerity. I spent my whole life judging other people. I thought I knew what was right for them without having a clue what was right for myself. If I'd paid more attention to how I felt, it might not have taken me fifty years to start enjoying myself." And just like that, the steam left my engine of righteousness.

Tyler was right—dead right—while Pam and our hand-wringing circle of friends were perfectly wrong. My business. Your business. God's business. The rest was sheer presumption. The rest was more about us than him. My job as a friend was to cheer Tyler on; if I couldn't do that, it was best to zip a lip and mind my own business. And what about our long-ago promise to watch each other's back? Did Tyler even remember our vow not to be age inappropriate, to protect our pride and our reputations? Maybe I'll ask him one of these days, if this satyr phase of his life ever passes. As for Pam, she's still beside herself, outraged by Tyler's new image, outraged that he is not behaving as she believes somebody ought to behave, and scared of what lies ahead for him if he doesn't button up and shut up. I wish she'd keep her eye on the ball and figure out why she has stopped dating, herself. It might just remove the sting from her bite.

⬛⬛▶ CONSIDER THIS:

❶ Do you believe your friends' lives are your business?
If so, why? How do they respond to your interference?

_____

_____

_____

_____

_____

❷ When you feel judged, how does this affect your
feelings toward the judgmental friend?

_____

_____

_____

_____

_____

❸ Do you talk behind friends' backs, as Pam has done
here?

_____

_____

_____

_____

_____

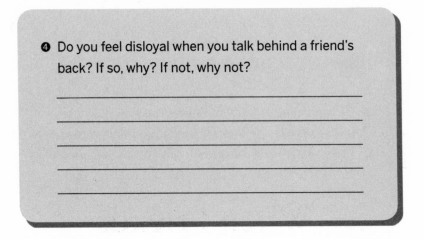

❹ Do you feel disloyal when you talk behind a friend's
back? If so, why? If not, why not?

_____

_____

_____

_____

_____

THREE

When Friends
Get Rich

Penelope was not an envious person. That is what she told herself. At thirty-six, Penelope was satisfied with her life as a midlevel editor at the women's magazine where she had been hired straight out of college. She was not a person who "lived to work"—Penelope never had been—but, rather, a person who "worked to live" as a way of helping her husband support their family, which had always come first. Penelope had made her choices—to be a mom, create a beautiful home, cultivate a happy marriage—and these priorities overshadowed whatever ambition Penelope might have had, once upon a time, to apply her journalistic skills to writing more than puff pieces about polka dots ("the new stripes") and colon cleansers designed to taste like chocolate blackout cake (and sugarless!). Penelope did not waste her time thinking about the roads *not* taken, the superior jobs *not* applied for, or ideas for books she had *not* pursued. She wasn't a dreamer, and never had been; Penelope didn't see the value in it. Instead, she preferred a steady paycheck and a circular driveway in Westchester to the risks, disappointment, bitterness, poverty, and substance abuse that appeared to come with a writer's life, which Penelope felt she had dodged like a bullet.

She admitted this to her friend Barbara, a novelist who lived in godforsaken, rural squalor with a herd of cats and a boyfriend named Stan who played the sax for weddings, bar mitzvahs, and high school reunions. "I admire you," Penelope told Barbara, who'd been working on the same murder mystery for years, throwing it in the trash, beginning again, despairing over ever getting it published. Barbara supported herself with odd jobs, lived without health insurance, hoped to have kids ("if I ever have time"), and made Stan promise that if she hit the big four-O without having published a book to make up for these poorhouse years, that he would have her euthanized. Barbara had not chosen to be so ambitious—she was, simply, born this way. Above the writing desk in the former woodshed she had converted into an office, Barbara posted a quote by Truman Capote: "When God hands you a gift, he also hands you a whip." Barbara could not ignore her gift. She flagellated herself for falling short but was constitutionally unable to give up the dream of seeing her work in print.

Penelope applauded Barbara's obsession, which allowed her the vicarious experience of being an artist without risking a run in her stockings. Penelope hated to see Barbara suffering, of course, but could not *not* be inspired by her friend's reckless, single-minded courage. She prayed that Barbara would find a publisher—at least that's what Penelope told herself—and was careful to conceal her pity beneath a veil of compassion, remaining staunchly supportive despite the fact that Barbara seemed destined for poverty. Each disaster in her life reassured Penelope that she had made the right choices (polka dots are better than food stamps), and that these choices would keep her safe, sane, and superior to her starry-eyed friend.

One ordinary Thursday morning, a phone call from Barbara exploded this assumption. Penelope was in her office, surrounded by swatches of jungle-themed maternity lingerie for the upcoming issue on "Tiger Mothers." Barbara was calling collect from a gas station pay phone because her home line had been disconnected (Barbara had never owned a cell phone). She sounded breathless, causing Penelope to expect the worst. Then Barbara started to sob.

"What's wrong, lamb chop?" Penelope asked, tacking on the special endearment she used in moments that might turn ugly.

"They bought it," Barbara whispered between sniffles. "I can't believe it!"

"Bought what?" Penelope asked.

"My book," Barbara said with disbelief. "And they want to make it into a movie!"

"You're kidding!"

"No!" Barbara stopped crying. Then she asked, "What do you mean, 'I'm kidding?'" Against Penelope's advice, Barbara had sent her unfinished manuscript to a second-tier literary agent nobody had ever heard of. Barbara was fed up with Penelope's caution. It wasn't her style to be so careful. For Barbara, life was all about risk. What mattered was what you risked *for*. Without telling Penelope, Barbara had cold-called the agent, described the novel's plot on the phone (middle-aged writer in the Hudson Valley murders her musician lover and sells his body parts on the organ black market, after which he haunts her and forces her to write a book about it before she leaps to her death on the Taconic Parkway), typed up a five-page synopsis, dropped the package at the agent's office, and was stunned when this agent called the next day to say he was sending the proposal to twelve different publishers. Within three days, half of the publishers wanted to buy the novel, sparking a bidding war. Barbara accepted a six-figure advance that was more money than Penelope had earned in her lifetime. But Penelope didn't know that yet.

"You don't sound happy," Barbara said.

"Of course, I'm happy," Penelope told her, digging her fingernails into her thigh. "Just surprised, that's all."

"And you'll never believe how much I got!" When Barbara revealed the sales figure, followed by the money she'd be getting for the film rights, Penelope felt bile rising up from her navel. She couldn't *not* be happy for her friend. But Barbara's sudden success *at what she loved*, that was the part that burned, made Penelope feel suddenly left out and worthless, a coward, an almost-ran. Barbara's

gamble turned out to be right, which made Penelope felt inexplicably *wrong*, filled with a longing she could not explain for something she did not believe she still wanted. This tempest of regret
and self-disappointment dowsed Penelope and pushed her down,
slumped, into her chair like a six-year-old who's just been slapped.

"Are you okay?" Barbara asked.

"Overjoyed. Speechless."

"You sure?"

"You deserve it."

"You sound weird."

"Work."

"I feel sorry for you having to go to an office."

Penelope restrained herself from screaming.

"I'll come take you to lunch next week," said Barbara. "We'll
celebrate. You always told me to stick with it!"

"That I did." Penelope hung up her office phone without so
much as saying good-bye.

Envy is a vicious parasite; it thrives on secrecy, darkness, and
malice. It sucks our best intentions dry and leaves us empty, vam-
pirical, sordid. "Envy is a form of hatred," says psychoanalyst
Polly Young-Eisendrath. "In jealousy, we want to possess something or someone that someone else has. In envy, we want to
kill them." Penelope did not want to hurt Barbara, but she didn't
quite want her to thrive, either. She needed Barbara to stay in her
place on the food chain—below Penelope—for her to feel good
about her own life. With Barbara's star rising, all of a sudden,
Penelope felt herself to be in descent, plunging into middle-age

domesticity with nothing more challenging in her daily suburban life than keeping the squirrels out of the drainpipes.

Envy reveals the shadows in friendship, the petty, selfish, insecure, grabby, ungenerous, mean, and competitive traits we all share. Misery loves company for a reason. "Envy is the great leveler," writes author Dorothy Sayers. "If it cannot level things up, it will level them down. Rather than have anyone happier than itself, it will see us all miserable together." At its extreme, envy turns to Schadenfreude, the bitter gloating we feel over envied people's failures. We applaud Bernard Madoff's perp walk in handcuffs not only because he was a crook but also because he was filthy rich. In friendship, envy runs amok. When our friends get rich, or successful, or, God forbid, famous, the force of envy is magnified as if on steroids, forcing us to confront shadowy elements of ourselves we wish did not exist. Envy is the shadow side of the American dream. "Competition, and by its corollary, invidious comparison," is "the "gasoline on which American capitalism runs," writes critic John Lahr. The dark side of wanting is aggression. Voracity. Craving. Hungry ghosthood.

If we cannot be happy for our friends, this is not friendship. This is common among frenemies caught in toxic competitions more rivalrous than loving. If we hope to forgive the people around us their happiness, we must be aware of the hungry ghost voice that does not want them to have more than we do. This is a universal law. Otherwise the void, the black hole inside you that never feels adequate, authentic, sufficient, worthy, pretty, wealthy, or tall enough becomes the dictator of your life and the bane of your successful friends' existence.

I know two friends like this. One of them got extremely famous. The other one never stopped blaming her for ditching her best friends, which she hadn't, as part of a guilt-exploitation game. This envious friend, a ne'er-do-well who rarely stopped blaming the world for his problems, located the famous friend's jugular, dug his teeth in, and never stopped sucking. He manipulated her with shame, and this toxic dance was hard to witness. The stakes kept getting higher and higher, till finally the envious friend, the parasite, began extorting money from the famous friend by way of emotional blackmail. "Charity begins at home," he would remind her when he could not pay his own rent. After that, she did pay his rent for most of a year, before his demands increased. After an enormous fight, when the parasite attempted to play the success card against her one too many times, the famous friend dropped him out of self-protection. From the couch of his studio apartment, he watches his famous friend on TV and wishes he could turn back the clock. But she refuses to speak to him.

Meanwhile, Penelope struggled with her demonic envy toward Barbara. As their lunch date approached, Penelope weathered the week from hell. For three straight days, she sank into the abyss that had opened inside her on hearing Barbara's excellent news. Penelope felt off balance, irritable, depressed, and lackluster at work, condescending toward her colleagues, and anxious to leave as early as possible. There were things at home that were bothering her, that needed attending to, which Penelope had ignored for too long in her la-di-da trance of self-satisfaction.

As the week wore on, she forced herself to attend to things that were bugging her at home, including a husband who made promises he didn't keep and kids who didn't appreciate her. Penelope began to feel a little better, and with this came glimpses of clarity. The discontent roused in her by envy was serving an okay purpose, she thought. And this book deal would be good for Penelope, too. Barbara would not be borrowing money. Barbara would be able to see a doctor, buy a cell phone, get a decent haircut, and stop with the SOS phone calls about wasting her life.

When Barbara arrived at the restaurant, she looked terrible. Frazzled, blotchy, underslept. Penelope expected her to lope in wearing Dolce & Gabbana, but Barbara was her usual, shlumpy self. Penelope asked her what was the matter.

Barbara had been up writing all night. The book deal, the money, had convinced her that if she did not begin working on something new right away she would be frozen in one-book wonderland. This thought made Barbara anxious and filled her with fear of writer's block. This anxiety then morphed into despair, which turned into a case of hives that was starting to erupt on Barbara's arms and hands. Barbara knew she was being ridiculous—she ought to be celebrating!—but was a mess. "I don't know what's wrong with me," she moaned. "Maybe I'm afraid of success."

Penelope breathed a sigh of relief. She had not lost her friend, Barbara, at all. Things would not be the same, but they would not be alien either. They were still themselves. Penelope was happy to be herself, and Barbara was still Barbara, with or without all that money. They talked about getting makeovers; Penelope ordered a vodka martini, and both of them had two. By the end of lunch, the two were loaded. Barbara and Penelope laughed so loud that the waiter offered them their check—early. Outside of Penelope's building, they hugged. Then Barbara pushed Penelope through the revolving door.

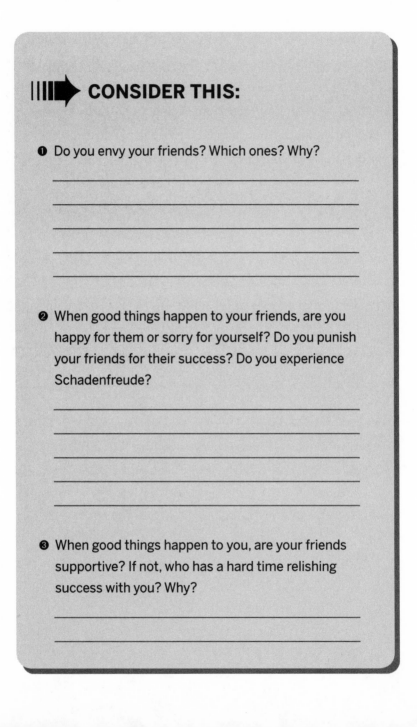

CONSIDER THIS:

❶ Do you envy your friends? Which ones? Why?

_____

_____

_____

_____

_____

❷ When good things happen to your friends, are you
  happy for them or sorry for yourself? Do you punish
  your friends for their success? Do you experience
  Schadenfreude?

_____

_____

_____

_____

_____

❸ When good things happen to you, are your friends
  supportive? If not, who has a hard time relishing
  success with you? Why?

_____

_____

_____

_____

_____

❹ Do you blame others for your personal choices?
Do you punish your friends for choices they make
that you do not agree with? Who and when?

_____

_____

_____

_____

_____

FOUR

Other People's Children

F elicia didn't mean to spy on Trevor. At least, that's what she told herself. Fifteen-year-old Trevor was the son of Felicia's friend, Tree, whose parents had been sequoia-hugging hippies who named their daughters after natural wonders. Tree's sister was named Waterfall. Her other sister was Moss. Felicia discovered Trevor's Facebook page accidentally, while vetting the page of her daughter, Tiffany, who was Facebook friends with Trevor.

Trevor's Facebook page shocked Felicia. It was a billboard of sex-crazed, dope-addled pranks; disgusting innuendo; and advertisements of apathy for all the Internet world to see. In one photo, Trevor had his mouth around the stem of an enormous bong, his eyes narrowed to glassy slits. In a webcast labeled *Mountain Dew+* Trevor was contorting himself on a bed, eyes popped out, high on a lot more than sugar-charged soda. In another photo, Trevor was bent over, holding the back of his pants, on the verge of mooning a pretty girl wearing only a towel. Felicia was taken aback by the filthy language and overcome by maternal protectiveness for this boy whom Felicia had known since birth. Something had to be done.

When Tiffany came home from school that day, Felicia—not wanting to give herself away—asked her moody, unpopular daughter how Trevor seemed to be doing at school. "He's gnarly," Tiffany told her between handfuls of Lucky Charms.

"Translate."

"Mad, bad, dangerous to know." Tiffany was obsessed with Romantic poetry and loved this description of Lord Byron, which captured exactly what Tiffany's elusive boyfriend would be like. "You know, Mom. Too cool for school."

"Popular?"

"Notorious."

This confirmed Felicia's worst fears, but she did not know how to tell Tree. Tree idolized her only child and believed that Trevor was a "pure soul." She attributed much of this purity to her own enlightened approach to rearing kids. As the daughter of protective if liberal parents, Tree embarked on single motherhood, following a one-night stand at an ashram, as an exercise in consciousness and "soul freedom." She followed the spiritual conviction that children should be adored, not disciplined, having chosen their parents before birth and come into the world as their guides and teachers. Tree thought of Trevor as her guru, which is why the boy told her what to do instead of the other way around. Trevor was never forced to sleep in a crib or wear clothes unless he was in the mood. He was allowed to run free like a feral child, to contradict his elders (Tree called this "finding his voice"), and play hooky from school whenever he wanted ("his energy is very *fluid*"). Enlightened parenting required that Tree trust her son even when he was lying and defend him even when he was wrong. Such terrible character-building lessons, combined with Tree's head-in-the-sand inattention, had resulted in Trevor's Facebook page, whose contents were driving Felicia crazy.

She suspected that Tree would never forgive her spying, but Felicia could not stop herself. Since Tree was such an ostrich, however, Felicia also felt justified in keeping an eye out for the boy. Then one day, Trevor went overboard. He was bragging about all the drugs he was taking. "Generation X, my babies. Poppin' and choppin'. Two pills," Felicia read, knowing that X stood for Ecstasy. Pot was one thing—Schedule II drugs were another. *Doing this in plain sight could damage Trevor long term,* thought Felicia, with companies scouring employees' online profiles during background checks. Or what if Trevor overdosed? How would Felicia live with herself? She had to speak to Tree or to Trevor, but which one would be worse? She stood at an ethical crossroads in friendship that had not occurred to Felicia before.

The matter of other people's children requires us to understand the supremacy of the parental bond. Friendship counts for
very little compared to the loyalty we feel for our kids. That is
why insights about our friends' children are almost always best
kept to ourselves. The exception to the rule is a case like Felicia's. When friends' children are in danger, loyalty requires that
we intervene. There's no fixed protocol for doing this, though,
and how we navigate these testy waters can spell the difference
between deepened trust and breaking up, as Felicia would soon
find out.

When a friend's child offended me badly, I learned this risky
lesson myself. Her daughter was a spoiled though talented girl
who had asked me for professional connections. I was happy to
hook her up with an employer who happened to owe me a favor.
This good man agreed to meet the daughter for lunch, in spite
of his overcrowded schedule, then waited in the restaurant for
half an hour before admitting that he had been stood up. Embarrassed, angry, and anxious to give this careless girl a sharp piece
of my mind, I sent her a stern e-mail. Rather than apologize for
her daughter's behavior, this friend accused me of breaching some
primordial law of parent-child-friend etiquette. My e-mail should
have gone through her, she insisted. What business did I have
bullying a child? I accused her of spoiling her daughter rotten and
preparing her poorly for the real world. She informed me that I
didn't know what I was talking about, being a childless person.
Since then, we hardly speak to each other. I regret this because
we used to have fun. Now, she seems to think I'm a bully. I had

broken a biological law—thou shalt never admonish a friend's kid—whose strictness I knew nothing about.

Human parents and their young share an intimacy unmatched anywhere else in the animal kingdom. This lifelong connection has fascinating roots in our species' evolution. When humans finally, permanently, stood up on their hind legs, moving from tree life to flat savanna ground, Homo sapiens developed much narrower hips in order to walk upright. With the woman's pelvis narrowed for walking, human babies needed to be born prematurely in order to squeeze their already enormous heads through the narrower passage. Whereas other mammals are born only when their brains are more or less ready to control their bodies, human babies can do nothing for themselves. Once out of the womb, these giant brains attached to helpless baby bodies need constant care, and this parental relationship—with its manipulations, give-and-take, and demands for justice, respect, and loyalty—becomes our ethical kindergarten. As parents, we are blinded by early dependency. Our children are forever babies to us, powerless, vulnerable, bobbleheads in need of our ferocious protection. This is not a relationship based on reason; nowhere are people less rational than on questions involving their precious brood. When friends complain about their children, it is tempting but dangerous to jump in with opinions they will likely hold against us later (just as we're wise to keep quiet when a friend bad-mouths a partner or spouse, even if we agree with them). In rare cases when friends request an honest opinion about their children, remember that less is always more and that your opinion will be taken *personally*. Rational as your parent-friend may seem, you will not be heard objectively, and the primitive feelings related to kin loyalty may be stronger than you anticipated.

Jeremy learned this when his friend Judd was having trouble with his teenage son. Judd's son, Zack, had entered that hellish adolescent corridor between puberty and emancipation—the zone known to many boys as teenager hell. Angry, aggressive, demonically disobedient—Zack had taken to covering his bedroom walls with graffiti and pornographic posters that Judd and his wife found highly offensive. When Judd tried talking "man-to-man" to Zack, his son refused to speak to him. Now Judd was at his wit's end with a marriage that was beginning to suffer. He wanted to talk to Jeremy about the situation at home and laid out the details, without holding back, one evening after work. "That kid is psycho," Judd said. "I was never crazy like that."

"That is one psycho boy you got!" said Jeremy with a laugh.

Judd stared at him and said, "He's not psycho."

"I just mean, he is kind of different."

Judd was becoming furious. Although Jeremy had done nothing but repeat his words back to him, Judd's rage was now directed at Jeremy. All the anger he'd been feeling toward Zack came rushing to the surface. Judd excused himself quickly and gave himself a quick talking-to, and cold-water face splash, in the bathroom. His rage had taken him by surprise. By the time Judd returned to the table, he had cooled down enough to hear Jeremy's voice as he apologized for speaking out of turn, and assured Judd that he was a great dad with a great kid that he should be proud of. In turn, Judd felt comfort in hearing his friend say this because he did not feel that way at the moment.

When Felicia finally told Tree what she knew, Tree was utterly devastated. Not because of the Ecstasy but because Felicia had spied on her son. Tree touched Felicia's hand with tears in her eyes and whispered something about spying being a sin, and that she'd been spied on by her own mother, and that friends did not behave this way. Felicia offered her apologies for delivering the news so abruptly but repeated her concerns that Trevor was jeopardizing his future with all this online information. Tree informed Felicia that she knew about Trevor's drug use and had told him to do "what felt right to him." At that moment, Felicia realized that Tree's moral universe was so different from hers that Felicia's rules did not apply there. She realized, too, that she no longer respected Tree. How could they be friends, Felicia wondered, without a foundation stone of respect? For her part, Tree understood that Felicia meant no harm but knew that, now, she could never trust her. How could Tree be a friend to such a busybody? Tree rose to her feet and turned to Felicia with a small bow, her palms together in the prayer sign, before walking mindfully toward her car. In her heart, Felicia knew that she'd done the right thing in a world where parents protected their children. In a world where parents worshipped them, maybe not.

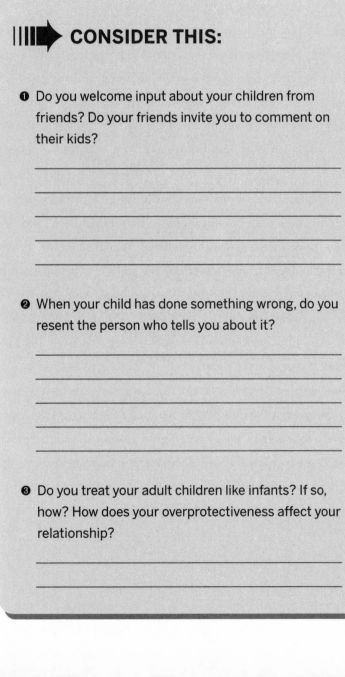

⫸ CONSIDER THIS:

❶ Do you welcome input about your children from
friends? Do your friends invite you to comment on
their kids?

_____

_____

_____

_____

_____

❷ When your child has done something wrong, do you
resent the person who tells you about it?

_____

_____

_____

_____

_____

❸ Do you treat your adult children like infants? If so,
how? How does your overprotectiveness affect your
relationship?

_____

_____

❹ If the minor child of a friend told you a secret about a potentially harmful situation, would you tell your friend? If not, why not?

FIVE

When Your Friend's Spouse Seduces You

Adriana was mortified. Earlier that evening, the husband of her friend Alice had made an obscene pass at her that left Adriana shocked and embarrassed, and forced her to leave Alice's house in a hurry.

Adriana was visiting Alice and her extremely good-looking husband, Ned, at the vineyard they managed in Napa Valley. There'd been too much wine for Adriana's taste from lunchtime on ("Oh, you must try this new Beaujolais!"), though Alice and Ned seemed accustomed to knocking back a glass or two before 12 noon. By the time dinner came and went, Alice and Ned were legally drunk and canoodling on the living room sofa while Adriana watched TV in the den. She could hear them giggling and slapping the wall and wished that they would go to bed. Then all of a sudden, before Adriana knew what had happened, Ned appeared in the den, collapsed on the couch beside her, lay his handsome head in her lap, and stayed there grinning up at Adriana, inebriated and amorous.

Surprised, Adriana was tipsy enough to allow Ned to stay where he was while the two of them watched TV, praying that Alice would not resurrect from her stupor. Adriana could smell Ned's aftershave (or was it his hair product?) and wished with all her failing willpower that she couldn't. Always a bridesmaid, never a bride, Adriana was unlucky in love and had watched enviously as Alice walked down the aisle to marry this Daniel Craig look-alike. Now here was Ned with his head in her lap, offering himself to her, sliding his big hand along Adriana's shinbone, sending chills up her too-tight spine.

"That tickles!" Adriana whispered, tipping Ned onto the floor and instructing him to be a good boy in a tone more amused than stern. She should have left at that precise moment; instead, Adriana lingered long enough for Ned to stand up, wrap his arms around her, yank her limp body against his, and plant a wet one on her waiting mouth. For three seconds (or was it ten?), Adriana allowed Ned to kiss her before finally pushing him away. "Okay, that's enough!" she declared loudly enough to snap Ned to his senses, cause Alice to stir on the couch, and make a beeline out the front door to her rental car.

Now, Adriana was in her room at the B&B, feeling angry, disgusted, and guilty, too, knowing that she had been flirting with Ned, while never encouraging such a crude pass. She was well aware of how Ned had been ogling her and did nothing to discourage his interest. Earlier that day, while Alice was preparing lunch, Ned offered her a tour of the wine cellar and Adriana knew perfectly well that his plan was to get her alone. She knew that when Ned brushed his shoulder against her breast (while pretending to look for the light switch), it was deliberate. Adriana did not resist Ned when he clutched her arm while going downstairs, and had giggled when Ned whispered "boo!" in her ear and rubbed his cheek on the nape of her neck. Adriana knew exactly what these gestures meant and, realizing her complicity, felt as much disgust for herself as she did offense over Ned's creepy moves.

Adriana hardly slept, lying awake for most of the night at the B&B, wondering just how far she might have gone if Alice had not heard her cry out, if Ned had pinned her against the wall, opened her blouse, proceeded to. . . . Adriana snapped herself out of the fantasy, disgusted to realize that, in a certain kind of mood, with enough Beaujolais under her belt, she could be *that* kind of woman herself, the type that other women could not trust not to prey on their handsome husbands.

The next morning, Adriana met Alice at the hiking trail as planned while Ned was doing his chores at the vineyard. Alice looked remarkably fresh for having consumed such a quantity and led Adriana up the stony walk to the summit of Orchard Loop Trail. Watching Alice bound up the hill in her khaki shorts, Adriana tried to keep up, feeling like the whore of Babylon. What should she do, Adriana wondered? Should she confess or should she say nothing? How could she look her friend in the eye without making some mention of this behavior? Adriana wasn't sure about the right thing to do—after the fact. Should a true friend fess up? Or was the information moot now that disaster had been averted?

As she trudged up the trail behind Alice, Adriana mused over how this might be different had she not been complicit in this flirtation? If she were to confess to Alice, on whom would she be tattling? Ned alone or both of them? What possible good could come from hurting her friend's feelings now? Watching Alice's strong legs carry her up the trail like a mountain goat, Adriana felt confused and evil, deeply shaken, like a stranger to her own moral boundaries.

Once they had reached the summit, Alice spread out their picnic breakfast and the two of them sat there, marveling at the vine-striped valley, hazy blue at this time of the morning. For several minutes, neither said a word, as if settling into the groove of a record before the music starts to play. It suddenly dawned on Adriana that Alice might already know what had happened! Ned could easily have made a midnight confession; Alice might already believe that Adriana had been a willing participant. Feeling sick to her stomach and miserably sorry, Adriana wondered if Alice was waiting for her to bring it up.

As if reading her mind, Alice turned to her and said, "Ned is *such* a naughty boy." Adriana smirked in agreement, but her expression was mixed with fear. "What?" asked Alice.

"Nothing," Adriana replied too quickly.

Alice cocked her head at Adriana, scrunching up her nose. "Why are you looking at me that way?" Adriana couldn't tell if Alice was baiting her or simply asking a question.

"What way?" Adriana asked.

Alice poked her hard in the arm. "You OK?"

"I'm fine."

"You're not fine," said Alice. "There's something you want to say." Alice leaned forward. "Isn't there?"

Adriana was a terrible liar. She had a face like a neon billboard. "Guys like Ned can get away with murder," Adriana said as nonchalantly as possible. "Imagine looking like that." Ned's beauty was an acknowledged fact, just like Alice's superior cooking. "It can't be easy," Adriana said, "getting everything you want."

"What do you mean by *that*?" asked Alice. "You think I'm a wimp?"

"No, I mean in general." Adriana attempted to backtrack. "For perfect people, I mean . . . people who look like Ned. It's bad for their character, being so pretty."

"You think Ned has a bad character?"

"I'm agreeing with you," Adriana said. "He's a naughty boy."

Alice was on her guard now. "What do *you* mean by 'naughty'?"

"What do you mean, what do I mean?" Adriana replied, struggling to sound confused. The air between them seemed booby-trapped, ready to blow. Then Adriana realized that Alice was simply hung over, her irritation stemming not from hidden knowledge but from an overburdened liver. Alice didn't know a thing; she was simply making lewd allusions to her husband. Adriana had invented the rest in her head. Now, she stood up and said, "I'm not used to drinking that much."

"You think I'm an alcoholic?" Alice asked from her place on the ground. In the bright morning sun, staring up with red eyes at her nervous friend, spider veins broken across her cheeks, Alice suddenly looked a lot like one.

"Please stand up, alcoholic," Adriana said, offering Alice a hand. "So this alcoholic can find a bathroom!" Alice pulled herself up, dusted off her behind, grabbed Adriana's arm, and the two friends went barreling down the path, leaving their cryptic conversation behind.

Ned greeted them at the vineyard's front gate. He was wearing sailor pants, combat boots, and nothing else. "Hello, Tarzan," Alice said, pounding on his chest and kissing him. Ned winked at Adriana over his wife's head. Adriana stuck her tongue out at him—which was silly, she knew, but the most contempt she could muster. When Ned tried to corner Adriana in the pool house later that afternoon, offering to dry her with his towel, she threatened to tell Alice if Ned came one step closer. Ned got the hint, shrugged, and left Adriana shivering next to the dinghy and flippers. When she left the next morning, her virtue intact, Adriana knew that she would never again flirt with the partner of someone she knew, or anyone coupled for that matter. It was too easy to lead them (and oneself) to temptation. As if they needed encouragement.

Sex and marriage can be unhappy bedfellows. It's cliché to speak about conjugal "bed death," when partnered people stop having sex, or monogamous people begin craving variation to jump-start their stalled mojo. This dynamic is rooted in what has been called our "predictably irrational" nature (which we will discuss in a later chapter). What makes sense to us *emotionally* does not necessarily make sense to us *erotically*, and this disconnect often causes confusion between married couples and their friends. Sexual nature thrives on uncertainty, risk-taking, and paradox: emotional components that do not necessarily make for happy marriages. "Passion in a relationship is commensurate to how much uncertainty you can tolerate," as Tony Robbins puts it.

We often become too predictable to our spouses and cause desire to wilt. "Sexual desire does not obey the laws that maintain peace and contentment between partners," psychologist Esther Perel writes in her superb book *Mating in Captivity*. "Reason, understanding, compassion, and camaraderie are the handmaidens of a close harmonious relationship," Perel notes. "But sex often evokes unreasoning obsession rather than thoughtful judgment, and selfish desire rather than altruistic consideration. [The] components of passion do not necessarily nurture intimacy," she concludes. "Desire operates along its own trajectory."

Since this trajectory is so unpredictable, we must err on the side of caution when spending time with married friends. Taboo desire has a stronger hold on us than we may realize. Believing intermarital flirting to be safe, we conveniently ignore how susceptible married people are to outside attention. For interlopers, flirting with the spouses of friends may be tempting for a number of reasons. Being lusted after is hard to resist, for starters. If we happen to be angry, or competitive, with a particular friend, aggressing on the spouse may be equally tempting.

For others, like Lucas, there was a predatory thrill in seducing other people's lovers. Lucas had no qualms about interloping. His greatest aphrodisiac rush was a flirtatious look from a friend's wife or girlfriend. Once attraction had been established, Lucas was hooked and would pursue the woman till the deed was done (or he had had his face slapped). He did not feel guilty for being a slime bag. Like bike thieves who blame riders who don't bother locking up their equipment, Lucas blamed his friends for not satisfying their women. Lucas was happy to take up where his husband-friends fell short. Usually, these trysts were brief—once, twice, three times at the most—then Lucas would grow weary of his conquest and end the affair on pretense of respecting the friend. The seduced wives and girlfriends felt wanted by Lucas, so their sexual egos were left intact. As for the friendships, Lucas would be forced to withdraw for a time until the wife or girlfriend cooled down, but he liked to tell himself that no close friend was ever hurt.

Desire is its own defense for a cad like Lucas. "I'm a man, I can't help it," he told himself, actually believing that tired old story. Lucas did not believe that sex was a serious thing. To him, erotic entertainment was play, a divertissement. Lucas had trained as a pastry chef in Paris, where it is not uncommon for lovers to be seen as necessary to marital happiness for wives and husbands both. Lucas chuckled at the newspaper story in which the wife of an international playboy (arrested in the United States for raping a maid) called her philandering husband a *chaud lapin* (hot rabbit) and suggested that moralists mind their own business. This is what Lucas believed, too. By making a friend's wife feel desirable, he was actually helping his friend by unleashing the wife's very own *chaude lapine*. It was a win-win-win, the way Lucas saw it. Then he met Roberto's wife, Vanna.

Roberto and Lucas had gone to patisserie school together. When Roberto was single, he and Lucas had double-dated, sharing stories about their amorous conquests. More than once, Lucas hit on the woman in whom Roberto was interested, imagining that Roberto never knew about it. After graduating, Roberto stayed in Paris when Lucas returned to the States. Then Roberto appeared with his new wife, Vanna, a tanorexic, onetime beauty with silicone breasts and a mouth like a truck driver. Lucas was half fascinated, half revolted by Vanna's vulgarity. He felt sorry for her, actually, for trying so hard to hold onto her withering beauty. She was so obviously insecure, and horny, that Lucas's merciful soul was awakened, and he found himself responding to Vanna's hot looks when Roberto was in the other room. What did it hurt, Lucas asked himself, when Vanna took his arm and squeezed, and sighed, and told Lucas he looked like a nasty little boy? He was making a woman feel good about herself. Besides, Vanna was still attractive in a sadly long-in-the-tooth kind of way. Roberto treated her with condescension, thought Lucas, and did not appear to be deeply in love with her. But Vanna was just wild about Roberto, which made Lucas want to help her betray her husband.

The cruise to Guadalajara came out of nowhere. Roberto presented Lucas with a free ticket ("three for the price of two!"), which is how Lucas found himself on a southbound freighter out of Long Beach one Friday afternoon. Vanna was in seventh heaven. Lucas felt embarrassed by her flagrant attention toward him, but Roberto didn't seem to mind at all. His not minding gave Lucas an eerie feeling and took the fun out of flirting with Vanna. Lucas noticed how Roberto left the room when Vanna started flirting—after happy hour the first day of the cruise—and did not return for a good long while. Lucas allowed Vanna to hug him when Roberto wasn't there, watching the door with trepidation. It seemed odd that Vanna was being so aggressive while Roberto was so hands-off. Till Vanna let Lucas know that this all was a setup.

"He doesn't care!" Vanna said, waving cynically toward the doorway. "I think he'd like to watch."

Lucas felt like a trapped animal, knowing that the joke was on him. Vanna and Roberto had lured him onto this Mexican love boat with the intention of spicing up their marriage (which was far too new to be so spiceless). Lucas was a pawn, a marital aid; any desire he might have had to sleep with Vanna vanished completely, replaced by the need to escape. But doing so might cause offense. Vanna kissed him on the nose and excused herself to freshen up in the bathroom. Lucas fled the cabin with his shirt untucked and found refuge in a chair by the Jacuzzi. He thought about Vanna and Roberto planning this seduction without his knowledge and felt positively sickened. It offended Lucas deeply to know that he had been so deceived. *Humiliating*, that was the word, Lucas thought as he imagined them sizing him up, the filthy, premeditated brazenness of it. How could people be so coarse? Lucas recognized the coarseness of his own bad behavior, obviously, but that was different. He was single. He wasn't consciously choosing, with his wife's permission, another man for her to sleep with! That was disgusting. Wasn't it? Lucas wasn't sure what he thought anymore as he sat there by the steaming water, tourist heads bobbing above its surface, and questioned his attitude toward sex. He did not know what was right or wrong. He only knew that he felt sick and that this disgust must mean something.

When Vanna found Lucas, she was furious. She dragged him to a place on the upper deck and accused him of having led her on. "I did nothing of the kind," he protested, vainly. Roberto appeared at that moment, locked his arm around Vanna's waist, and wondered where Lucas had disappeared to so fast without even a polite good-bye to his wife, whom he had deeply offended. Lucas found himself in the ridiculous position of explaining to a friend why he had not seduced his wife, which was crazy, but Vanna demanded an explanation. "You think I'm not good enough for you?" she asked.

"I don't know what you're talking about."

"You have to come out here and stare at the coeds?" said Vanna.

Roberto stared dangerously at Lucas before pulling his wife back down the hall to their cabin. Lucas spent the rest of the night on deck, waking up the next morning to the adobe glare of Guadalajara going full throttle. Vanna and Roberto were already off the boat by the time Lucas made his way to his cabin, relieved to have them off his tail, relieved to spend the day by himself. That night, the couple kept to themselves, and Lucas lost $350 at the craps table. When the croupier took his final pile of chips, Lucas bid his fellow players good night instead of going to the cash machine for more. He was tired of always going for more. Lucas was tired of himself.

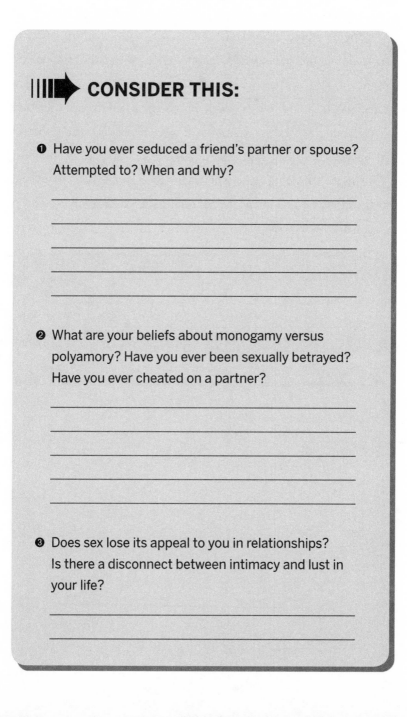

CONSIDER THIS:

❶ Have you ever seduced a friend's partner or spouse? Attempted to? When and why?

_____

_____

_____

_____

_____

❷ What are your beliefs about monogamy versus polyamory? Have you ever been sexually betrayed? Have you ever cheated on a partner?

_____

_____

_____

_____

❸ Does sex lose its appeal to you in relationships? Is there a disconnect between intimacy and lust in your life?

_____

_____

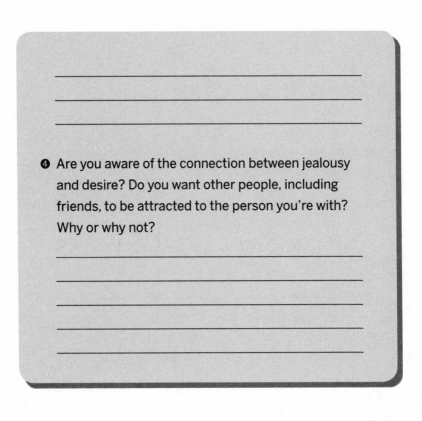

❹ Are you aware of the connection between jealousy
   and desire? Do you want other people, including
   friends, to be attracted to the person you're with?
   Why or why not?

SIX

Spongers and Users

A ngie was a con artist who looked like an angel. Blond as Botticelli's *Venus*, ethereally pretty, softly spoken, and with no visible means of support, she floated into my circle of friends a few years back and, with targeted precision, befriended, deceived, and exploited half a dozen of my closest buddies, one by one. By the time each one realized what had happened, it was already too late. Seduced by Angie's appearance of friendship, they opened their wallets, homes, and networks in the belief that their love was returned. Only afterward, comparing notes, did they realize just how deluded they'd been.

Angie was a sociopath. Sociopaths are individuals willing to say or do anything to attain their selfish objectives. In the mind of a sociopath, the ends justify the means regardless of who gets hurt. Manipulative and ethically bankrupt, sociopathic behavior is marked by "a pervasive pattern of disregard for, or violation of, the rights of others." They display false emotions (known as "shallow affect" by psychologists), grandiosity, deceptiveness, superficial charm, lack of empathy or remorse, and—most conspicuously in Angie's case—a parasitic lifestyle. Angie was eerily cold and self-justifying. She would ask to crash on someone's sofa ("Two weeks, I promise") and, because she looked like Uma Thurman, people didn't tend to mind—till a month had gone by and they could not get rid of her. Angie was always destitute and, to make matters worse, wore a permanent crown of martyrdom for a tragedy that befell her years before, whose pathos she milked like a witch's teat. Machiavelli would have loved Angie.

Spongers, mooches, con artists, and cheaters elicit moral outrage for two primary reasons. First, their dishonesty insults our intelligence. Second, their unfairness and nonreciprocity offend hardwired morality. Humans have survived in groups only through reciprocation, paying generosity forward, and punishing sociopaths like Angie who refuse to give back. Indeed, the social brain's ability to detect nonreciprocators—the small percentage of people in any group who'll always attempt to exploit others for their own gain—is among our most primitive design features. Whether we're hunter-gatherers living on the savanna, or executives on Wall Street, the cerebral cortex is running particular software for social contracts and precautions. We do this via an "exchange organ" in the brain that keeps track of fairness—not a literal organ but different neurons and tissues working together to do a single job. Determinations of right and wrong are based on tallies made by this exchange organ of favors received and given, generosity compensated or not, status attained or refused: the arithmetic of perceived personal justice.

This is why the Golden Rule is the single principle on which all spiritual traditions have managed to agree:

"What thou avoidest suffering thyself seek not to impose on others." (Epictetus)

"Do to every man as thou wouldst have him do to thee; and do not unto another thou wouldst not have done to thee." (Confucius)

"One who, while himself seeking happiness, oppresses with violence other beings who also desire happiness, will not attain happiness hereafter." (Buddha)

"Do not seek revenge or bear a grudge against one of your people, but love your neighbor as yourself." (Judaism)

"And as ye would that men should do to you, do ye also to them likewise." (Christianity)

"One should never do that to another which one regards as injurious to one's own self." (Hinduism)

"Hurt no one so that no one may hurt you." (Islam)

"Regard your neighbor's gain as your own gain, and your neighbor's loss as your own loss." (Taoism)

The problem is that it's much harder to apply tough justice ("out with the nonreciprocators!") to real people in our actual lives when they're soaking us dry. There are few things harder to ask a friend than, "Do you really think I'm picking the check up *again?*" I knew a woman who drove me to the brink this way. Every single time we met, this platonic friend would excuse herself to go to the little girl's room the second the check hit the table. This did not merely annoy me—her prefeminist presumption outraged me, in fact, as a friend as well as a man. An entire book should be written about the double standards between men and women (men grouse about this constantly)—the ways in which a certain kind of woman will play on a guy's sexist chivalry while demanding equality when it doesn't cost her. This particular person was one of those women, and it wasn't ever going to change. To avoid the discomfort of bringing this up, I broke off our less-than-close acquaintance.

Moral outrage can easily blossom into victimhood and self-righteousness, however. There are no victims in the mooch game, strictly speaking; often, we offer users our necks and say "Suck!"; without a host there can be no vampire. Also, it is naïve to imagine, in fact, that so-called victims gain no satisfaction from their crosses and nails. Howard was a guy like that. Howard was like St. Sebastian waiting to happen, chronically attracted to men who'd bleed him dry and make him look like a saint. These men never reciprocated, enabling Howard to pine, lust, and shell out the money (rent loan, prison bail, haircuts, you name it) like a doormat with a pin number and a broken heart. Howard lived for this feeling of self-exploitation; acting like a victim made him feel alive. There are a lot of people with this masochistic fetish. Unrequited desire and pain are their emotional cocktail of choice. When this addiction exists between friends, the symbiosis between host and parasite can be so seamless that it's impossible to say exactly who is using whom.

Mooching includes a wide range of behaviors: disappearing when the bill arrives, calling only when you need something, targeting friends for favors without telling them, riding friends' coattails for personal gain, sleeping with their spouses, taking advantage of their loyalty toward us in times of need. Mutual exploitation is a part of friendship (though, we hope, not the main part) and is only a problem when friends don't give back. Helping and being helped is how love shows itself between people. Just as we need to sponge sometimes, we also need to be generous. It feels good to offer assistance.

Oxytocin, the hormone of love and connection, is produced when the brain is tickled this way. By extending ourselves, we are elevated; withholding our gratitude, we are diminished. Mooches like Angie believe they are profiting at friends' expense, when, in fact, they're deceiving themselves, depriving themselves of what matters most: relationships with people who know they can trust you; self-respect based on playing fair; the experience of shared generosity, mutual care, and doing no harm. For all her ingenuity, Angie was deprived of these things and is one of the saddest, most desolate people I have ever known. My friends have not seen her in quite a while. The last thing we heard (on the Internet), Angie was hoping that a woman she'd met would offer her an apartment in Paris. If she could only find a car to drive till then. And maybe even a place to live.

||||➡ CONSIDER THIS:

❶ Do you reciprocate in your friendships?

_____
_____
_____
_____
_____

❷ Do you have spongers and users in your life? If so, who and why?

_____
_____
_____
_____
_____

❸ Can you ask friends for favors without feeling guilty? Are you generous when asked by others?

_____
_____
_____
_____
_____

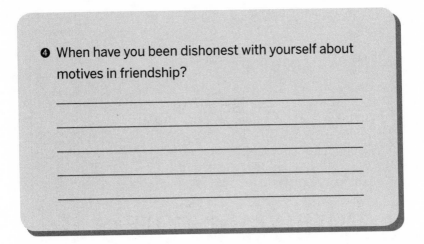

❹ When have you been dishonest with yourself about motives in friendship?

_____

_____

_____

_____

_____

SEVEN

Forgive or Forget It

Doris and Cleo were having a fight. The problem centered on a stray cat that Cleo's son, Noah, was keeping in the apartment he'd sublet from Doris—in spite of the antipet terms of the lease. Doris, a hypochondriac who was also allergic to cat hair, was furious by this breach of contract, though she had no intention of ever returning to the apartment where Noah was living. Jamie, a mutual friend of both women, was doing her best to persuade Doris to let the grievance go, in order to keep the peace with Cleo, who was highly protective of her son.

"This could end your friendship," Jamie was saying. "What's the big deal?"

"I have allergies!" said Doris. "My throat could close up. I could *die!*"

"But you're never going to live there again."

"That's not the point. He broke our agreement. It's wrong," Doris said in a huff. Logic had nothing to do with it. Doris was, in her own mind, already in the ER, strapped to a gurney with an oxygen mask over her face, seconds away from a horrible death, all because Noah was spoiled rotten. "I'm throwing him out—"

Jamie told her that Cleo, overprotective of her son, would never forgive her. The friendship was worth more than a cat. But reason could not talk Doris down from her ledge of self-righteousness.

Cleo called Jamie that afternoon. "This is the last straw," she told her.

Jamie told her that it was between Noah and Doris. "He's a big boy."

"He's my son!"

"It's a cat problem."

"Exactly," said Cleo. "It's not World War III."

"He broke the agreement," Jamie said before stopping herself.

"Whose side are you on?" asked Cleo.

Jamie decided to butt out. You've seen those moments in war movies when the enemy sides are marching toward each other in slow motion and impact cannot be avoided? That's how Jamie felt with Cleo and Doris. Her friends were locked in a battle they could not back down from. Helpless, Jamie watched in disbelief as their twenty-year friendship moved to a climax over a calico kitten. Doris and Cleo could find no way forward without forgiveness. But how that might happen remained unclear.

How do we forgive our friends? How do we back down once we are seized by rage, or gripped by the urge to fight or flee? Though humans are *rationis capax*—capable of being reasonable—we vastly underestimate the power of emotion to blind us. We also overestimate the power of reason to save us from precipitous action once our primitive emotional centers have been hijacked. We know the reasonable path with our heads but are pulled toward destruction by our feelings. At war within ourselves between what we know and what we feel, we nearly always follow our feelings, which are nearly always self-protective and prone to anticipating pain. This is known as the negativity bias. Once burned, we expect to be burned again. In survival terms, it's better to be safe than sorry, which is why we tend to hold onto grudges in spite of the compassionate voice in our minds whispering "reason, empathy, kindness, peace." Psychologists use a circus analogy to describe this imbalance between power and emotion. Our emotions are like a wayward elephant, they tell us. Rationality is like the tiny rider on its back, kicking like crazy, wielding its stick, trying to steer the beast here and there. This is why forgiveness is so hard. We are straddling an emotional pachyderm. Once its feelings are hurt, or we have been violated, our primitive nature opposes approaching where we have been wounded.

We bandy the word "forgiveness" around without fully appreciating its complexity. "We talk about forgiveness as if it were one thing, but we should really talk about *forgivenesses*," says Helen

Whitney, whose documentary film, *Forgiveness: A Time to Love and a Time to Hate*, examines this thorny issue. "Forgiveness is not always the best policy," says Whitney. "Sometimes forgiveness can be bad for your health." She is mostly talking about heinous, violent crimes, but the point is well taken. We dumb down forgiveness into a Hallmark card and expect it to come automatically (just like love on Valentine's Day), but that isn't how it really happens.

Jane and Victoria had reached a crisis in their friendship where forgiveness seemed out of reach. Jane's lying, evasion, and years of not doing what she promised had pushed Victoria to her limit. These old friends had been planning a working trip to Umbria, where they would photograph beautiful things to be sold to magazines. Victoria initiated the trip and requested time off from her teaching job at an art school because Jane had expressed an interest in traveling together. Now, Jane refused to book her ticket. The charade between them had gone on for months. The deadline for fare discounts was about to pass and Victoria was waiting for Jane. Then Jane went MIA for a week, failed to return Victoria's increasingly angry phone calls, and eventually sent an e-mail, claiming to be too broke to go and expressing how sorry she was to crap out at the last minute.

Victoria was beside herself. It wasn't just the missed vacation (Victoria did not like traveling alone). It was the breach of trust, first of all. The disappointment, second. And then the chain reaction set off by Jane's mutiny, a painful linking of feeling abandoned to the loneliness of Victoria's single life, then to her self-dissatisfaction, then to her restlessness, and finally to anger at herself for giving up on photography as a livelihood in favor of spending her days critiquing the fledgling work of kids rich enough to get into the art school where she taught. This trip with Jane was meant to shore up her faith in herself as a creative artist. Instead, Victoria felt doubly bad being stationary, hearing her mother's voice ("A woman alone, that's a sad thing"), which took her down lovelorn alley and the story of herself as unwantable. This rancid chain of discontents tightened around Victoria's neck till she could hardly breathe; till the missed trip was the least of it, and Victoria saw Jane as her nemesis, the nonfriend who rubbed her nose in her personal pile of self-loathing.

It did not matter that Jane was telling the truth. She had spent much of the previous month agonizing over how to keep her promise. But Jane would have maxed out her credit card to pay for the airfare. Instead, she made the difficult decision—prompted by a coffee klatch with her sponsor from Debtors Anonymous— to work her program, tell the truth—finally—and make amends later if possible. She had not hurt Victoria on purpose; her worst offenses were unemployment and not communicating the truth earlier. Still, Victoria was treating her like a villain, filtering Jane's image through the lens of her own self-loathing.

We do this all the time. We all live inside our own movie, where the angles, lights, and music are different from everyone else's. We paint the world with our own desires like Cecil B. DeMille constructing a film set. We step in and out of each other's frame but are acting for our own director even when we are together, seeing through our own prejudices, history, longing, regret, and idealism how we wish things were. Victoria could no more appreciate Jane's recovery film than Jane could step into Victoria's road flick. This failure to communicate rendered forgiveness impossible for them. At least for the moment.

We can overcome resistance to forgiveness by remembering that we do it for ourselves. This is an important point. Saturated in thinking of forgiveness as something that we do for others—or because it is right—we resist it when we are hurt or angry. Attempting forgiveness, we puff ourselves up into cartoons of selflessness that fail because we're being inauthentic. This is why the forgiveness process stalls, pretending to be generous for others' sakes—or to do the right thing—when our guts and minds are still seething.

To forgive authentically—to open our hearts to those who've wounded us in the past—we must first acknowledge that it is a self-serving act in the most intelligent, dignified sense. Holding on to resentment is like swallowing poison and waiting for the other person to die. We stay angry out of spite but the enemy party has long since moved on. It's just us here with our Prilosec and therapy bills, eating ourselves up alive. A Holocaust survivor, Edith Eva Eger, put it well: "You must be strong to forgive," she wrote. "Forgiveness is not about condoning or excusing. Forgiveness has nothing to do with justice. Forgiving is a selfish act to free yourself from being controlled by your past."

In the end, Cleo and Doris circumvented the cat business. They valued their friendship too much to sacrifice it to their shared neuroses. Noah had no intention of getting rid of the cat and would sooner have moved out of Doris's apartment than cave in to her unreasonable order. Cleo supported him in this decision, regardless of the sublet terms, since Doris lived 300 miles away. Doris, seeing that she had been trumped, withdrew into an angry pout, and the two of them stayed silent for three months. Finally, at Cleo's insistence, they had dinner and decided, through clenched teeth, to agree to disagree and not bring up the subject again. To make this story more ridiculous, Noah, who has commitment issues, ended up sending the cat away with a girl he no longer wanted to date. Doris was vindicated; her long-distance lungs breathed a sigh of relief. Cleo did not have to back down, and Jamie saw her friends reunited. It wasn't the perfect kind of forgiveness, being helped along by circumstance. But it was the one that kept them together.

Victoria and Jane never spoke again.

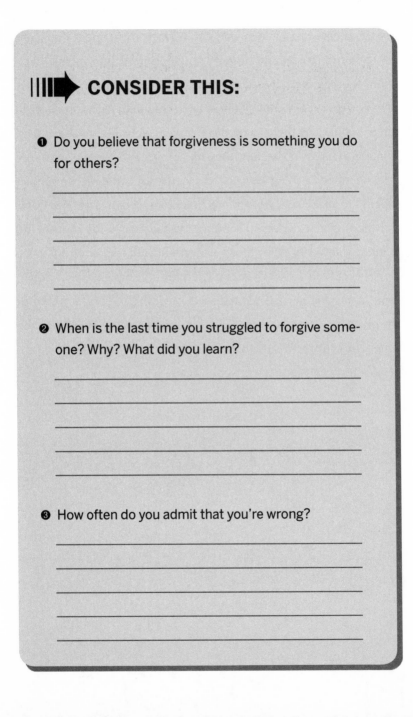

CONSIDER THIS:

❶ Do you believe that forgiveness is something you do for others?

_____

_____

_____

_____

_____

❷ When is the last time you struggled to forgive someone? Why? What did you learn?

_____

_____

_____

_____

_____

❸ How often do you admit that you're wrong?

_____

_____

_____

_____

_____

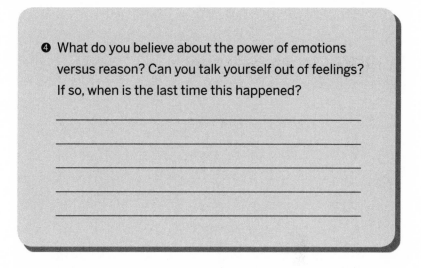

❹ What do you believe about the power of emotions versus reason? Can you talk yourself out of feelings? If so, when is the last time this happened?

_____

_____

_____

_____

_____

EIGHT

The Eros
of Friendship

E very friend is a lover, too. Not sexual lovers, necessarily, unless friends are playing it fast and loose, which usually spells the end of the friendship. Lovers in the sense of a shared bond related to passion, or life's work, or secrets. Sometimes, the shared bond is a wound or a common enemy, and other times it's a strange mutuality bordering on romantic attraction yet aimed at something beyond one another. Many close friendships begin with romantic feelings, although we don't like to admit it. We're confused by intense emotions that feel, sporadically, *more* than platonic and may or may not include physical attraction. Witness the rise of the bromance. Try getting between the gals on *Sex and the City*, who worship their cosmopolitan coven.

Dishonest with ourselves about erotic feelings (erotic *does not* mean sexual), we often hide the truth from our friends. We deny the cravings we feel for them, how we pine for them like Tristan and Iseult, the inordinate, contradictory feelings that friendship should not prompt, say our minds, but often does. We feel deep attraction toward our best friends. We long for each other's company. We crave specific things from one another. This explains the variety of close friends a person can know at any one time. All of us have a myriad of internal chambers, and each has its own taste for company. We cleave to friends for a sense of completeness, affirmation, belonging, and love; for memories to honor and promises to keep; for intimacy in its numerous colors, stopping short of the bedroom door. Friendship has fewer conditions than erotic love. With lovers, we may be nipping and tucking, behaving, fitting to play a role of desirability. We are often more comfortable with our friends, more able to be ourselves, than with our lovers, and this is how it's meant to be. The roles we play with our lovers have very specific parameters. We make trade-offs for physical intimacy that are not required with our friends, any more than we require friends to tell us we're attractive, crave our bodies, or gaze at us in wonder across the glow of candlelight.

Friends differ from erotic lovers in key ways, but in others they are identical. Take jealousy, one of Eros's worst demons. The possessiveness that corrals our lovers is the same one that tries to lasso our friends. In romantic love, jealousy may lead to sex, giving it some added value and meaning. In friendship, jealousy has no outlet aside from withdrawal and licking of wounds, the humiliating awareness (in the jealous friend) of having wandered into the wrong movie. I've loved many friends in my life, sometimes disproportionately, even passionately, and with every single one of them, I've had to learn a degree of restraint.

Agnes and I fell in love the day we met. She was wearing a beret because her hair was dirty, and sat hunched across from me at a coffee shop for an interview set up by her boyfriend, whom I had met at a conference. Agnes and I bonded over our shared artistic ambitions, as well as over traumas from our past, with the rapid, wall-dropping fervor of people falling in romantic love. Our attraction was palpable, gleeful, intense, and circumscribed by our commitments to other people. The absence of sex only made the heat stronger. We were free to flirt without any danger, infusing our marathon "mind melds" with gobs of seduction, the pure delight of platonic friends who can heap unabashed adoration on each other's head without risk ("I love you more!" "No, I love you more!"), satisfying the need for devotion without the comedown of having to make it work.

I loved Agnes ferociously, more than any romantic partner I'd known till that time, and she claimed to feel the same about me. We wrote love notes and talked on the phone every morning. We saved special clippings and books for each other, shared Thanksgivings, vacations, a shrink. I obsessed about her when she was away and was thrilled—too happy probably—each time

I saw her. During a transatlantic flight scare, when her plane fell thousands of feet in the air and Agnes thought (she told me later) that this might be it, her life flashed in front of her eyes. She sat there doing an inventory of all the things she was grateful for in her life, and being my friend, having me in her life, was actually on her short list. This convinced me that we were sweethearts of the soul—married in spirit—and plunged me yet further into a welter of feeling too complicated for friendship but somehow uncontrollable. Of course, I did not want to control it.

There's a reason that Eros, that mischievous god, was believed by the Greeks to be the brother of Chaos. The ancients understood the chaotic power of all forms of love to leave us disheveled, unbalanced, and broken. Erotic desire is fierce and wild; the love of friends is more familial (as in healthy families), contained, unconditional, balanced, and tame. But when friendship becomes both familial and wild, we have a dangerous animal on our hands. It is not all that different with friends, except that the object of desire should not be each other. Friends stand side by side, not looking into each other's eyes as lovers do, but outward and upward to common interests. This is the boundary that Agnes and I had been crossing, blurring our purpose, confusing our passion. We didn't want to sleep together. We wanted to have a vision together, to work together, change the world together, encourage each other in art and romance. Like many friends who are smitten, we mistook these signals and fell into erotic patterns that nearly ended the friendship. When we focus our love craving at our friends (even when we have romantic partners), we threaten the integrity of friendship and enter into a dangerous liaison.

This is not to say that sex between friends never works. A friend of the family, whom I will call Martha, sleeps with her best friend and ex-college roommate every time she visits Portland, Oregon. Russell, the ex, is single and a womanizer, but a charming one whose company and body Martha enjoys. When they are not having decadent getaways at Russell's house on Crater Lake, he is taking care of the IT for Martha's flower business in Toronto. They are on the phone five times a week (more than many boyfriends and girlfriends I know) but are not in love with one another. They share an intense, common interest—escape— and erotic compatibility. Martha has never had "a scintilla of angst" over her triannual sleepovers with rough-and-tumble Russell. Now and then, grownups can handle arrangements that beggar belief for less evolved people, like those of us with jealousy issues. But this is the rare exception.

Most of us need not to sleep where we eat, to keep the erotic in friendship at bay. Luckily, Agnes and I are still close. After a period of relative distance (mutually agreed upon due to my infantile jealousy), we rebooted our bond and put our deep friendship back on its proper footing. Now, when Agnes tells me about her men, I feel happy, not jealous, and truly hope she will find happiness with someone who's worthy of her, someone who can bridge the chaos of Eros and be a true friend to her as well—a man who'll look into her eyes but who also stands at her side, taking in the world together. A lover can do that. A friend cannot.

CONSIDER THIS:

❶ How many of your friendships began as romantic attractions?

_____
_____
_____
_____
_____

❷ How does attraction to friends affect the friendship?

_____
_____
_____
_____
_____

❸ How does jealousy play into your friendships? Are possessiveness or competitiveness problematic for you?

_____
_____
_____
_____
_____

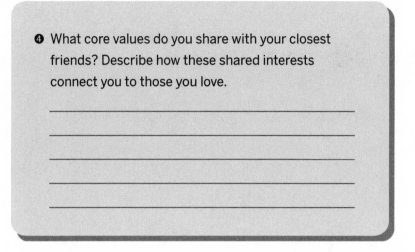

❹ What core values do you share with your closest
friends? Describe how these shared interests
connect you to those you love.

_____

_____

_____

_____

_____

NINE

Let's Connect
(But Not Really)

Gretchen was an Internet junkie. Isolated in the wilds of Teaneck, New Jersey, desperate for a social life, this thirty-four-year-old homemaker spent too many of her waking hours in front of a computer screen, chumming with people she would never meet, expanding her web of virtual friendships.

Gretchen's MySpace page overflowed with messages from around the world ("It's Becka from New Zealand! What up, Chickie?????") that helped her feel more cosmopolitan. Online, her soccer mom life was elevated from one in which Gretchen felt like a sidekick (disinterested teenage sons, workaholic husband) to an existence where *she* was the main event, attracting instant messages from Auckland, must-see links from Dallas, and even a sexual proposition from a lesbian in Madrid whom Gretchen accidentally "poked" in a chat room.

This online habit thrived, as do all addictions, on denial and secrecy. Gretchen told herself that virtual friends were better than no friends at all. What did it matter that she'd never actually met these people, shaken their hands, or could tell them apart in a police lineup? The point was that she was *connecting*, thought Gretchen, which was more interesting than watching reality TV, or eating Cheez Doodles till she was big as a house like Dottie, her poor neighbor who moped around in her muu-muu and couldn't be bothered to wash her hair.

For Gretchen, it seemed wonderful "knowing" people so unlike herself. It was refreshing being part of their lives and sharing, vicariously, in their struggles. Awakened one night by the ping of her e-mail, Gretchen spent hours IM-ing with Kiri, who was going through a bad divorce, talking her "friend" down from acting in a way she might regret. Just before dawn, feeling flushed and happy, Gretchen crawled back into bed with her husband, happy to lie next to a warm, breathing body. When her husband asked Gretchen where she had been, she lied that the cat had gotten out. Her husband's buying this story was proof of the fact that her online friends knew more about her than he did. Everyone on her MySpace page knew that Puck—the Persian cat she had adopted—was agoraphobic.

Gretchen felt increasingly torn between her flesh-and-blood life and her online persona. Like an alcoholic cheating on a spouse, Gretchen discovered that her intoxicating virtual relationships made everyday Teaneck seem sober and dull. "OMG," she posted one day, "I wish that I could LIVE here!" meaning with her online crew.

"LMAO!" replied Axle Rider in Duluth. "You can. Sort of."

"Here here!" posted Peaches and Cream, who identified herself as a libertarian cashier in Las Vegas.

The three of them shared a cyber-laugh that left Gretchen feeling even lonelier in New Jersey with her traumatized cat, her missing family, and an empty date book. As the gap between her two worlds continued to grow, Gretchen felt less connected still to her husband and kids, and her real-life friends, most of whom lived in other towns. This disconnect caused Gretchen to resent her real life even more and herself for being marooned inside it. It confused her that she had the illusion of closeness, even intimacy, with these online entities, while actually "having" these friendships alone. Meeting on the Internet had the power to bring people close—but rarely close enough. Cyberspace allowed friends to connect—but not really. Like Pyramis and Thisbe, mythological lovers forced to communicate through a chink in a wall, virtual intimates never quite touch. There are glimmers of closeness, flares of emotion (or rather, emoticons), phantom gestures of care and support, but all without an ounce of substance. In between the chat room sessions, MySpace mashups, and Facebook IMs, Gretchen was increasingly aware of how illusory the Web really was, and what a hopeless enterprise seeking connection online actually was.

Virtual reality is not our friend when it comes to emotional life. In our twittering age of e-mail, text messages, and social media sites such as Facebook, the emotional traps of virtual blindness can be tricky. Empathy is a face-to-face business after all. Our brains are not yet wired for deep connection divorced from physical exposure. In face-to-face interactions, one study showed, 55 percent of the emotional meaning of a message is expressed through facial, postural, and gestural means; 38 percent through the tone of voice; and only 7 percent through words. It's far easier to abuse, or lie to, profiles of disembodied entities changing their virtual monikers with a click of a mouse than it is not to care about real human beings. Virtual reality actually halts the feedback channel that our brain relies on as a way of anticipating other people's needs, and the impact our actions will have on them. Free from face-to-face interaction, ethical behavior risks cyberfree fall.

E-mail has changed profoundly how we bond, connect, inform, deceive, and distance ourselves from those we care about. It is easier to lie in an e-mail than by almost any other means (far easier than in an actual letter, which feels so *substantial*). This point became obvious to me recently due to the e-mail lying of my friend Chip. I have known Chip for twenty-five years. I can read his mood from a hundred yards away, which is why, when Chip wants to cancel a date for questionable reasons (we both cancel a lot, to be fair), he always sends a same-day, "sore throat" e-mail.

Chip would never pretend to be sick to my face—or even on the telephone. He'd feel shame lying where I could see or hear him, knowing that I could blow his cover. On e-mail, however, he lies right and left (as many people do). Chip's a solid friend and a straight shooter in real life. But on the Internet? I wouldn't trust him for a minute.

We share ourselves en masse on social media sites with a captive audience of countless others, exposing our personal lives and enjoying the exhibitionist buzz. But how our friends display themselves online (as Pam learned with Tyler's womanizing) may contradict how we know them in the flesh. Self-aggrandizement, misrepresentation, and narcissistic overkill are rampant. A serious-minded woman I know shares more glamorous self-portraits on her Facebook wall than anyone who isn't a model (or a hooker) has any sensible reason to post. Another friend shares the most tedious details of his day with hundreds of "friends" for reasons that completely escape me. No one cares that he wolfed down a pint of Chunky Monkey, nicked himself shaving with a disposable, *looooves* the TV show *Mad Men*, or has a crush on CNN's Erin Burnett. Still, he continues to regale the immediate world with the minutiae of his singular existence.

Our unprecedented ability to self-advertise to countless strangers we call friends has altered our notions of private versus public and the terms, therefore, of friendship itself. Habitués of social sites seem to forget that information shared with everyone loses its meaning and carries little value between close friends. They forget that friendship is forged by exclusivity, specialness, and the particular, close-to-the-heart, off-the-record sharing that can only happen one-on-one. Friendship thrives in private places circled by trust and seeded by time. Promiscuous friendship, like promiscuous sex, only grows shallower over time, offering diminished returns. Neglecting the difference between private and public can be devastating to friendship, in fact, as a reader from Portland made clear in an outraged letter:

"I was close to not speaking to Florence anymore. We barely talked and I didn't trust her. She no longer seemed sincere to me. The façade she created online was a joke, first of all. She lied about her private life constantly. She built herself up to seem happy, successful, and popular (her goal was to have 5,000 FB friends). If I'd been a jerk, I could have outed her, crashed her virtual world down, but I didn't. One night, we were supposed to get together for a drink and Florence canceled at the last minute. To be honest, I was very hurt. I had told her how much I was looking forward to seeing her. You know what she had the nerve to tell me? 'Just read my Facebook page. It's all there.' That was it. Our friendship was over for me."

It is alienating, and sometimes insulting, when friends forget that privacy matters. It hurts to be lumped in with online strangers. Our friends may feel devalued, unseen, and unloved. That's why we need to be on guard against letting the Internet come between us and the people we care about. The next time that you are with a friend and can't keep your eyes off the smart phone screen, turn the stupid thing off. Try to be mindful of how technology may be compromising your ability to connect in real time;

and why you care more about an incoming text or IM than you do about present company. Gretchen was forced to learn this lesson the hard way. After two addictive years of cyber-bingeing, at her family's request, Gretchen forced herself offline, cold turkey, canceled her MySpace account, and found a therapist to talk to about feeling lonely. Gretchen pressured herself to join a gym, where she happened to run into a neighbor, Rebecca, who invited her to go for power walks in the morning together. Their growing friendship is not exciting. It does not offer Gretchen escape from her life. She learns about neither Auckland nor Hong Kong. Instead, they talk about life in Teaneck, their absentee husbands, perimenopause, and the ridiculous price of heirloom tomatoes. One recent morning, Dottie appeared at Gretchen's door and asked if she could join her and Rebecca on their walks. Now the three of them are power marching around the neighborhood, five days a week, in their leggings and headbands, carrying their three-pound weights. Gretchen will never love Teaneck, she tells them. She isn't a suburban girl at heart. But at least it's starting to feel like home.

||||➤ CONSIDER THIS:

❶ Do you avoid friends using e-mail or other technology? If so, when and how?

_____

_____

_____

_____

_____

❷ Do you misrepresent yourself online? If so, why and how?

_____

_____

_____

_____

_____

❸ How does insecurity play itself out in your online life?

_____

_____

_____

_____

_____

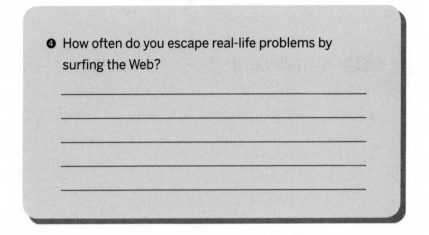

❹ How often do you escape real-life problems by
surfing the Web?

_____

_____

_____

_____

_____

TEN

A Colleague Isn't a Friend

olleagues are not friends. This may be hard to admit when we're feeling a rush of fondness for those we work with, or want to work with, or are competing with, or wish to join forces with in our march toward success. Just as we may mistake friends for lovers, the lines between friendship and collegiality are easily overlooked, trespassed, denied, and disobeyed. But there are differences. Friends are people we choose to love. Colleagues are chosen for us by circumstance, relationships created in the public sphere.

Friends don't belong to the public sphere. Friends want our messy interior, the offstage self, the self without walls. Friends want to know what's unacceptable in us, the warts we hide, the heartbreak, the bloating, the "us" that slumps out of bed in the morning, the person we are before assembling our worldly armor. Friends know your weaknesses, failures, and downside; they feel closer to you because of these imperfections, since you have seen their underside, too. Friends reveal themselves during shut-in times and allow one another to peer beneath the social persona, trusting each other not to reject the raw footage. It's in these falling-down, off-the-record moments that intimacy happens. Your friends are never impressed by you—you cannot impress them, they know you too well—and this is a great relief. In a culture running on fossil fuel, sucrose, and unemployment, friends are those with whom you're free to feel lazy, lumpy, cranky, and full of hot air—the ones you grow old with, and obsolete, without losing your cherished simpatico.

Colleagues are there for the public sphere. They're the people you care about impressing, bound to you conditionally and for reasons not dependent on love. This does not mean that we can't love our colleagues; some of my dearest acquaintances are work-related. Still, I know they are not my friends. I like to call them New York Friends, even when they're not in New York. New York Friends define themselves through infrequency, distance, and pragmatism. New York Friendships can take place wherever people are bound through ambition, competition, e-mail, constant contact, and survival needs. This competition need not be career-related. Neighbors are a type of colleague, for instance, bound to us in the public sphere by role, reputation, and convenience. We keep up appearances for our neighbors, compete for the snazziest garden or pool, and guard against too much self-revelation lest our secrets seep into the neighborhood. When we marry, members of the in-law family become our domestic colleagues, piggybacked to our marital status. With rare exception, they'll cut themselves off (like work friends who no longer work together) when the marriage ends. Following a breakup, they distance themselves, automatically choosing sides, remaining in touch only awkwardly like coworkers when you get fired. For colleagues, when the role's obsolete, the connection is, too, and you're left—if you failed to grasp the distinction—clutching a sign that reads I THOUGHT WE WERE FRIENDS!

Just as sleeping with friends will leave you confused, becoming too attached to colleagues will put you at risk for pain and betrayal. This may come as a rude awakening. You may feel as if you've been thoroughly duped when you, in fact, have duped yourself. It's easy to be fooled this way. Being gullible myself, I have often mistaken colleagues for friends. Then an ugly experience woke me up. Sondra was a colleague whom I revered. Although we became involved in business, we first met socially and began having lunch on a semiregular basis. Sondra was fun and smart and unemployed; she was also well known in the publishing business, which I was not aware of when we met. Despite warnings from people who knew her in business, I believed that we were real friends, that the Sondra whom I was growing to love was the real Sondra. I hadn't yet faced the importance of context in human relationships and the frightening, inarguable truth that each of us is actually more than one person.

Though we like to believe that we have a consistent personality across time and space, psychologists tell us that this isn't true. We'll return to Sondra in a moment. Human personality is more like Play-Doh than it is a chunk of granite. We all change our "self" on a regular basis and have a talented Mr. Ripley inside us. We're not quite the same person at the office as we are at home. We're different when we're bustling through a market than while making love, and different when we drink with friends versus when we're lost and alone in a foreign city. Moving from one situation to the next, embodying various roles, we adjust definitions of right and wrong and what others may expect of us. We define ourselves through situations, meaning that when you encounter a person, you are never meeting a full identity. You are meeting the "self" they choose to display against a particular backdrop. As psychologist Philip Zimbardo puts it, "We are *where* we live, eat, work, and make love." We make these mercurial character shifts with frightening ease. In a book called *Snakes in Suits* by Paul Babiak and Robert D. Hare, we learn that "Many traits that may be desirable in a corporate context, such as ruthlessness, lack of social conscience, and single-minded devotion to success, would be considered psychopathic outside of it."

This brings us back to my colleague "friend" Sondra, and my wake-up call when she went back to work. In a pants suit, this woman turned into a snake. I was shocked by the coldhearted

change in her. Suddenly, I was a writer to her, rather than a con-
fidant. Returned to a role of power, Sondra stopped being the
person I knew and morphed into her role. When a project of
ours did not work out, she stopped speaking to me. Never before
had I seen so clearly that colleagues are conditional intimates
at best. Sondra's shape-shift left me holding the sign that read I
THOUGHT WE WERE FRIENDS! I was wounded at first, then
outraged, then sad, and finally wiser for the rejection.

An acquaintance named Brenda had a similar crash. Brenda is
a thirty-eight-year-old tax accountant from Miami who prides
herself on being a people person. Outgoing, sincere, and eager
to make friends, Brenda is the type of woman who returns from
every vacation with a crew of new acquaintances she stays in
touch with afterward. Brenda believes that connection is the key
to life and knows no greater pleasure than expanding her dossier
of people. Since we sat next to each other on an airplane a few
years back, I've received biannual shout-outs from this bubbly
lady. After reading a blog that I wrote about colleagues versus
friends, Brenda weighed in with a similar experience:

> I liked what you said about losing your innocence. That's exactly
> what happened to me. My best friend from work, this guy named
> James, basically saved my life for the past three years at this horrible
> company we both hate (but can't quit in this economy). You know
> how close you can get to somebody at work? We ate lunch together,
> carpooled together, bitched about the boss together. We both love
> classical music and went to the symphony together a few times. I

trusted James completely and would have told you two weeks ago
that we were friends for life. Then the Fed Ex debacle happened.
He had asked me to mail something for him from my department
because this company's so absurdly cheap that they count how many
stamps we use. It was a personal item (I didn't ask what), but instead
of putting it in the Fed Ex pile, like he asked me to, I decided to
fly under the radar with snail mail. The package got flagged in the
mailroom for being too heavy; in fact, it was a marijuana vaporizer
(!) that James was sending to a friend in Berkeley and using me as a
mule. You would think that I'd be the one to get mad, right? Wrong!
They X-rayed the box, gave it back to me, I made up something
about it being a box camera (!), opened it, and gave it back to James.
Rather than being contrite, he blamed me for not using Fed Ex, told
me that this would change our office relationship, and it would be
best if we no longer knew one another. Just like that. Now, when
he sees me in the cafeteria, he won't even look at me. At first, I
was very upset! Then I got disillusioned, which is why I wrote to
you. I remember what you said about losing your innocence when
you realized that colleagues are rarely true friends. I figured that you
would understand. I realize now that we were using each other to
survive this miserable job. It was a "relationship" based on convenience. And that's not a genuine basis for friendship.

Often, we fall into relationships without questioning their
foundation. In the case of colleagues, this is a mistake. Friendship demands that we're radically honest and unsentimental
about the context, intention, and nature of our emotional con-

nections. Wisdom comes from accepting relationships *as they are* and maintaining appropriate boundaries and expectations. Right relationship is difficult but indispensable. The situation with Sondra was disappointing and useful, leaving me more honest about professional bonding and all forms of public intimacy. It made me cherish more than ever those off-the-grid, entirely personal friendships where neither party is playing a role, or getting ahead, or watching his back, or caring where you work, live, or to whom you are married. Friendship is not conditional. It does not rely on form to function.

CONSIDER THIS:

❶ Friendships belong to the private sphere, collegial relationships to the public one. It's a mistake to confuse the two kinds of connections.

_____

_____

_____

_____

_____

❷ Are there colleagues in your life whom you mistakenly call friends?

_____

_____

_____

_____

❸ Do you consciously practice right relationship? Are you able to gauge candor appropriately, or do you reveal too much? If so, where and how?

_____

_____

❹ Are you honest with yourself about your intentions in so-called friendship? If not, with whom are you being insincere?

ELEVEN

Frenemy Territory

Molly and Paula were peas in a pod. These ambitious, intelligent, controlling women had been best friends since their sophomore year in college. After graduation, they backpacked around Europe together, became passionate about the same social causes, attracted the same breed of men (couch potatoes), and climbed shoulder to shoulder to the top of the heap in their respective professions.

Molly and Paula were the best of friends, except when the other one wasn't around. When Molly was absent, Paula habitually backbit against her beneath a mask of fawning concern ("If only she could stick to a diet!"), revealing Molly's secrets and sorrows to anybody willing to listen ("You didn't know about the implants? Oops!"). Whenever Paula was out of earshot, Molly highlighted her lapses in personal grooming ("Groucho Marx would have killed for that mustache") and focused on tearing down Paula's achievements. They were the best of friends when they were together, saboteurs when they were apart. They gave mutual friends emotional whiplash.

Molly and Paula were frenemies. Their path to this ambivalent juncture had run something like this. As standoffish, lonely, strong-minded sophomores, Molly and Paula were initially drawn together as narcissistic havens of refuge, islands of mutual reflection where each one could be seen, if not fully loved, by a female peer with kindred issues. While disliking aspects of each other from the start, these antipathies seemed unimportant compared to their similarities. Not until Molly and Paula were isolated in Europe together did the thorns of malice sharpen to nails and affection twist into passive-aggression. Without either of them noticing, Molly and Paula, apparent best friends, had transmogrified into frenemies.

This masquerade continued for years until Molly finally crossed the line. It's a well-known fact among friends (and enemies) that if you want to stick it to someone, *really*, the most effective means of FU is ingratiating yourself to their exes (particularly if they no longer speak). Feeling especially wicked, Molly did exactly this with Seymour, Paula's despised ex-husband. Unbeknownst to Paula, Seymour and Molly were still in touch, so when Seymour needed a dog sitter (for the French bulldog Paula had given him), he asked Molly if she could lend a hand. Molly, who liked animals more than people, jumped at the chance to irritate Paula and agreed to take care of Iggi for Seymour. It wasn't the poor dog's fault if his parents couldn't act like adults, Molly reasoned. And though the dog was a sore spot for Paula, which Molly knew better than anyone, it was high time for Paula to get over herself! Molly did not bother consulting with Paula before becoming Iggi's caretaker. The offending gauntlet had been thrown.

For Lester and Harry, the frenemy conflict began quite differently. These childhood buddies grew up on the same street, played together in Little League, and double-dated all through high school. On one of these double dates, Lester brought Lisa, a glasses-wearing strawberry blond who promptly took a liking to Harry. Lester, who looked like Conan O'Brien, made a gentleman's agreement with Harry the jock that he was free to court Lisa since Lester had only been out with her once. Harry made a date with Lisa within thirty minutes. Stewing in his hormonal juices, Lester seethed; knowing that Harry gave Lisa a go-steady ring, Lester went testosteronic; his chest-pounding aggression could not be calmed. This was poisoning his love for Harry; it also made Lester hate himself for having agreed to this devil's bargain. Harry, for his part, refused to feel guilty for taking Lester at his word, and this indignation caused Harry to withdraw. Their friendship now hung by a brittle thread, and neither knew what to do to save it.

These frenemy scenarios may seem extreme—and extremely unlikely to find resolution—but most of us have frenemy bonds in our lives whether we admit it or not. The friend who has an extra hard time being happy for you when good things happen. The buddy who never completely approves of important choices you make in your life. The peer who finds something nasty to say about issues that are dear to you, all too often and with too much enthusiasm. These contradictions in friendship are confusing enough that we do our best to deny them, allowing frenemies to stay too close, for too long, and cause more damage than may be necessary. For frenemies do cause damage—physical damage— and having them in our lives is bad for our health.

When we realize how permeable we are energetically and neuronally, frenemy life takes on a whole new level of toxicity. Dan Goleman, the author of *Emotional Intelligence*, explained to me how this contagion of emotion happens, and why each of us needs to beware of individuals who secretly wish us ill. "We're forming brain-to-brain bridges, all the time, with the people around us," Dan told me during our talk for *Ethical Wisdom*. "We catch each other's emotions like a cold. The people we love are our biological allies."

Biological allies?

"If we're in a relationship with people who are constantly putting us down, or people in a distressed or toxic state, that has *biological* consequences," Dan insisted. "If we're around people who are nourishing, warm, and put us in a positive state, that has different biological consequences." In contact with loved ones, our bodies secrete oxytocin and endorphins, while chronically distressing relationships reverse that process, suppressing the immune system and raising stress hormones.

"The importance of a particular relationship in your life will determine the power that each encounter with that person will have for you. If your boss is in a bad mood," he said, "that can upset you in a way that no one else's mood can because you place more importance on what the boss does or says. You attune to them more, which makes their emotion pass to you more strongly."

When frenemies are up close and personal, they can undermine us in ways we might not notice, as Molly and Paula had been doing for years. As contradictory creatures—inconsistent, uneven, and deeply flawed—we may excuse a bit too much contradiction in those around us. Friendship magnifies contradiction in our emotional landscape, as do all forms of intimacy. Each of us is changed and revealed by caring; that's why people who fear their own contradictions tend to avoid intimate connection, which is guaranteed to blow their cover. Instead of admitting the truth to ourselves—that each of us houses a Tower of Babel, including antagonistic, frustrated, unharmonious emotions that make no rational sense—a motley crew of conflicting desires, competitive thrusts, and natural aggression—we spend our lives keeping up the appearance of being less contradictory than we are. We pretend to be strangers to our own complexity and misrepresent ourselves to our friends. And they may be doing the same to us.

Molly and Paula had a happy ending—although it came by traumatic means. Four months after the Iggi incident, Molly was diagnosed with early-stage breast cancer one September morning at a clinic near Paula's office. They had not spoken in all that time. Molly left the doctor's office, drove automatically to where Paula was working, walked into her office, told her the news, and the old story ended. With Molly's mortality on the line, Paula's anger over Seymour seemed inconsequential. This generosity roused Molly's shame over deliberately hurting Paula, and the two of them had a cry-fest over what supreme bitches they both had been.

Molly and Paula had been genuinely dear friends once, before unspoken truths suffocated the air between them and they became biological enemies. Now, with life and death at stake, Molly and Paula rediscovered their love for each other. Paula helped Molly through her recovery. Molly told Seymour to buzz off and peddle his French bulldog elsewhere. Seymour left Iggi on Paula's doorstep with a note, "I couldn't live without you," tied to his collar with a pink ribbon. In turn, Paula gave Iggi to Molly, who liked the slobbery dog more than she did, and Iggi gave Molly oxytocin rushes to help through the chemotherapy.

Lester and Harry went their separate ways. When Lisa and Harry got engaged, Lester took a job in California to avoid their happiness. He couldn't get over the ancient wound, the blow to his masculinity. A man's best friend isn't his dog, after all. It's his libido.

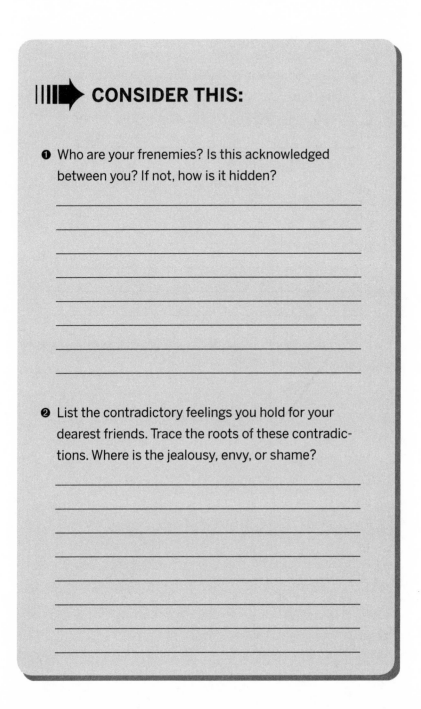

IIII➡ CONSIDER THIS:

❶ Who are your frenemies? Is this acknowledged
between you? If not, how is it hidden?

_____

_____

_____

_____

_____

_____

_____

❷ List the contradictory feelings you hold for your
dearest friends. Trace the roots of these contradictions. Where is the jealousy, envy, or shame?

_____

_____

_____

_____

_____

_____

_____

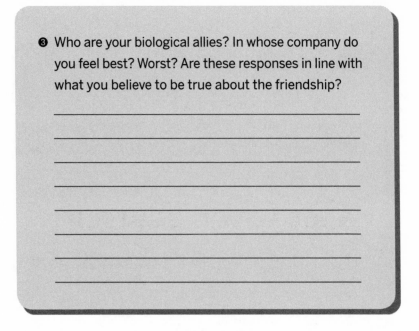

❸ Who are your biological allies? In whose company do you feel best? Worst? Are these responses in line with what you believe to be true about the friendship?

TWELVE

Get Over Yourself

Leila is a difficult woman. She may be the most difficult person I've ever known. Truly difficult people share one tragic flaw: They have no clear lens upon themselves. They do not know how crazy they are. Leila's an almost impossible nut to crack. Blind to her own ulterior motives, needy beyond reason, unfiltered, solipsistic, and critical, she's the bitch in the market who says something nasty just because she's PMS-ing. Leila pisses off cab drivers, waitresses, telephone operators, and other service personnel on a regular basis, snidely, believing she's always right. When Leila isn't being passive-aggressive, she's just being aggressive.

She is also amazing, wonderful, and fun. She's a brilliant artist brimming with *joie de vivre*, amplified wonder, tremendous thirst for knowledge and surprise. Her favorite adjective is "devastating," as in "that van Gogh, it was *devastating*." She lives for being devastated. Leila's a highly educated, good time–loving, trust fund–secured, obsessive artist and woman about town. She is also, always, forever single. At fifty-six, she has never been married and never had children. She is painfully, chronically, permanently lonely and believes that nobody understands what it's like to be as alone as she is. Narcissists can't see the suffering of others, which is why being friends with them can be so lonely. Leila has almost no awareness of her effect upon others.

And she wonders why people have always dumped her. Like me. I dumped her. I could not take it.

Being friends with such people—the toxic-myopics—the ones who spew but can't see their own sputum—can be torture. She's inflexible because she believes she is right and believes, incorrigibly, against reason, in the infallibility of her own choices, even when she's full of shit. Inflexibility is another narcissistic pitfall. Leila's rigidness was a product of fear. Fear of being abandoned. Fear of failure. Fear of solitude. Fear of illness. Fear of poverty. Fear of insects. The list goes on and on. Her fears make her stubborn, which shuts the world out, leaving Leila to wonder why people leave her. Walled inside her myopia, she expects the world, including her friends, to mold themselves to her needs.

How many friends have you known who turned away from each other out of fear of change? How many people have you lost in your life because you could not get over yourself? I know a Jewish man who never forgave his best friend for converting to Christianity. The friend had fallen in love with a gentile woman who would only marry him if they were the same religion. As a nonpracticing Jew, he was okay with this, but his friend found the concept completely disgusting. To abandon your people for a shiksa girl? To raise your sons without a bar mitzvah? Their friendship ended over what seems like a none-of-your-business, grow-up, no-brainer thing—a get-over-yourself squabble over religion—but some people cannot bend. Friendship is an ongoing practice of transcending prejudice, willingness to be wrong, getting over what we think is right. It is the opposite of fear, which is why Leila has such a hard time changing. Instead, she plays the victim and refuses to get off her high horse, eat humble pie, make sincere amends with the people she's offended, and finally move on with her life. I truly hope that this will happen.

While writing this chapter, I changed my mind; or, rather, saw my hypocrisy clearly. I've been writing a chapter about getting over oneself in friendship while holding onto an old aversion. The truth is that I miss my friend, Leila. But I have been too inflexible to admit it. I've been holding on to old bitterness, the very thing I dislike in her, feeling righteous, superior, and vaguely stuck. I've been sitting here thinking about our history, the irreplaceable memories we've shared, since meeting all those years ago. And so, I decided to write her an e-mail, which I sent an hour ago. I didn't do Leila's inventory. I didn't pull guilt trips or anger or blame. Instead, I asked my friend how she is and told her that I'm thinking about her. I'm ready to get over it. Life is too short.

||||➡ CONSIDER THIS:

❶ Everybody makes mistakes. If you're looking for the perfect friend, you will die alone. Do you require perfection?

_____

_____

_____

_____

_____

❷ Nobody is 100 percent right in any altercation. Can you admit when you're wrong, and, if so, are you willing to change?

_____

_____

_____

_____

_____

❸ What are you inflexible about? How do these stubborn-as-a-mule stuck spots hold you back in your friendships?

_____

_____

_____

_____

_____

❹ Does fear interfere with your ability to care about others? Would you rather be safe or happy?

_____

_____

_____

_____

_____

THIRTEEN

The In Crowd

"One of the dominant elements [in life]," wrote C. S. Lewis, "is the desire to be inside the local Ring and the terror of being left outside." This desire to be an insider as opposed to an outsider, to be part of the chosen group rather than a friend of losers, is deeply woven into the tribe-loving human psyche and can prompt very bad behavior. "Of all the passions, the passion for the Inner Ring is the most skillful in making a man who is not yet a very bad man do very bad things," Lewis concludes.

There are few social blows more painful than expulsion from an inner circle, as I learned after my gossip drama with friends described in Chapter 1. This fear of humiliating, outsider status explains the willingness to be cruel in exchange for social acceptance. The cautionary tale of a woman named Tammy exemplifies this temptation to ethical weakness among social climbers. Tammy was obsessed with being accepted by people she considered "cool" but felt, chronically, like an outsider. She was, at twenty-nine, a miserable, self-absorbed advertising flunky in Oakland, California (*Not even San Francisco!* she'd think, gazing from her studio apartment window at the glittering city across the bay). The life that Tammy wanted always seemed to be somewhere else, available for truly popular people, unlike herself. Until she could find the magic entrance to this elusive world of "cool," Tammy would never be satisfied. She would never stop feeling like a hungry ghost. Hungry ghosts are those ravenous figures in Buddhist mythology (metaphors for the insatiable ego) condemned to eternal craving in a world of elusive satisfaction. Hungry ghosts symbolize that part of ourselves that never, ever has enough or feels truly satisfied with who we are. Each of us has at least one hungry ghost inside him or her, but poor Tammy commandeered a battalion, an army of starving zombies searching for entrée to the inner circle where she would finally feel as if she were *enough*.

Tammy was never okay being merely herself. She used bitter humor and condescension as shields against feeling insufficient, invisible, and inconsequential, inept at making intelligent choices, and ineligible for the kind of happiness that existed only for *them*, not her. There were few things that Tammy would not do in order to become one of *them*, including lie, suck up, and drink too much with idiotic men carrying invitations to private parties Tammy wanted to crash.

One dreary night, she found herself at the bar of a club called Zeke's, wondering how she might infiltrate the exclusive poker party being held at the proprietor's ritzy mansion after hours. Tammy had been coming to Zeke's for a month, but nobody seemed willing to give her a chance. She was telling this story to the bartender, Carla, hoping for some inside information. Carla seemed to know everyone's business. Though Carla wasn't part of the in crowd herself, Tammy had noticed that management liked her. Carla had whistle-blown her way onto Zeke's good side by reporting chronic theft by three of the waiters, she told Tammy in a whisper; still, being overweight and unglamorous, Carla was never invited to Zeke's poker party but didn't seem to mind a bit. "I'm not good enough for them," said cheerful Carla. "But guess what? I don't give two shits."

Well I do, thought Tammy. Anxiously, she awaited a chance to ingratiate herself to Zeke, a skinny Iranian who slithered around the club in snakeskin shoes, his comb-over dyed (or so it appeared) to match the tanning bed–orange of his complexion. No stiletto heel was too high, nor tube top too revealing, for Tammy to hoist as ammunition. Yet Zeke's attention would not be grabbed. Tammy was frantic to be noticed. Finally, a few weeks later, her chance to get a foot in the door presented itself unexpectedly. Having finished a double shift, and sucked down her third mojito, Carla made the mistake of confessing to Tammy

that she had been borrowing cash from the till in the form of
orders she never rang up. Carla planned to give every penny back,
she told Tammy, confiding that her finances were a disaster, especially raising a teenage daughter with no help from the deadbeat
dad. As Carla spoke, she began to cry, because it was back-to-
school time and she hadn't the measly funds to buy her daughter's
school supplies. "That's the only reason I did it," Carla assured her.

"Stealing is wrong."

"I know that. I'm planning to pay it back."

That's what they all say, Tammy thought. Staring at Carla with
her dripping eye makeup and bad haircut, Tammy wondered con-
temptuously how any woman with any self-respect could allow
herself to come to *this*. Tammy scarcely believed that she had
considered befriending a dishonest lowlife like Carla, and considered whether her loyalty ought not to be with Zeke, whose
establishment she liked and who was being robbed by yet
another self-excusing employee. Tammy found herself at an ethical crossroads: To betray an acquaintance, a single mom whose
only crime was lifting a hundred bucks from a Persian millionaire
who worked her for pennies; or to protect Carla, help her safe-
guard her job in order to give her daughter notebooks for school?
In Tammy's mind, there was no contest.

She buttonholed Zeke the following night as he angled through
the glitzy crowd. She whispered into his perfumed ear that she
had employee information. In Zeke's office, Tammy embellished
by saying that she'd seen Carla take the money. Zeke gave a sideways glance at Tammy's cleavage, thanked her for being a loyal

regular, and asked if she was a gambler. Tammy told Zeke she'd do anything for a game of five-card draw or some penny slots. Zeke handed her a card for the party next Friday.

That week, Carla was fired, and Tammy felt bad, but only for one day. On Friday night, she found herself at Zeke's tacky mansion, like Cinderella finally called to the ball while she was still cute. She found the party depressing and disgusting. Men were offered cocaine and lap dancers; women were offered attempted rape. Around midnight, after an hour of fighting off the grubby advances of Zeke's uncle, a seventy-year-old junk-metal millionaire, Tammy made her exit, feeling like yesterday's lunch. Why did she think that Zeke wasn't a sleazebag? Why were all the supposedly cool people such losers when Tammy got to know them? If there wasn't a popular group to get into, what was having friends all about? This made her think about Carla, which made Tammy feel even worse, because Carla was nice and Tammy had screwed her. For what? To smell an old man's bad breath all night and try to keep her sweater buttoned? As a cherry on this upside-down cake, Tammy discovered when she got home that all the cash in her purse was missing.

"The drive to form in-groups is always shadowed by the creation of out-groups, whose members are automatically less deserving of everything for no other reason than that they're not *us*," biologist E. O. Wilson writes. This is why the desire to be on the inside can be so morally debilitating. Consider the ritual of hazing. Young men will drink dog urine as the price of becoming a member. They will let themselves be humiliated, degraded, sickened, and spat upon for the gift of being inside the group.

Once inside, they will instantly be in conflict with everyone who isn't. That's because the price of loyalty to our own group is always aversion toward another.

Us-versus-them is our greatest ethical albatross. In human evolution, us-versus-them helped to save us from attacks by outsiders. Banding together to survive in a hostile environment with limited resources, our ancestors developed the irresistible urge to dichotomize people into opposing categories. We are only comfortable when the remainder of humanity may be labeled as *them*. This explains why there is only one type of universal human joke—what we call a Polish joke. "The Flemish have Walloon jokes, the English tell Irish jokes, the Hutu have Tutsi jokes and the people of Tokyo have jokes about the people of Osaka," journalist Lance Morrow reminds us. We think about each other in terms of teams. This was referred to by Sigmund Freud as "the narcissism of minor differences."

Teams, cliques, and inner circles form around charismatic leaders. When these leaders have enemies, friends may find themselves enlisted in gang warfare. Take the case of Andrew and Iaian, a couple of clique leaders born to be rivals at a midwestern university. On one side, you had freethinking Andrew and his motley crew of geeks, nerds, shlubs, and artists, both male and female, the smartest kids at the school. On the other side, you had Iaian's buttoned-down pack of uptight, full-of-themselves rich boys who lorded around campus in Brooks Brothers jackets, preparing themselves to rule the world.

Iaian's snubbing personality had spawned a whole clique of guys who got a kick out of being mean. The most obvious target was Andrew and his band of wild-haired, poorly washed geniuses. There was only one problem. Her name was Jemma. Jemma was one of the prettiest girls at school, a double major (premed, astrophysics), beloved by Iaian—and a devoted member of Andrew's group. This could-be prom queen much preferred hanging with the outcasts. Sharon and Anne, the only other girls in Andrew's group, had acne or dandruff (or both) and liked Greco-Roman poetry more than man-hunting or counting carbs, which bored the bejeezus out of Jemma, too. Jemma found men silly most of the time and suspected she might be a lesbian, someday, if she could meet a woman like Ellen DeGeneres. But coming out was decades away, if ever, and long after Jemma had given birth to at least two perfect, artificially administered, sperm donor babies.

Iaian worshipped Jemma and hated Andrew, which confused him. If a person you liked was inside a group you hated, where did you draw the line? If you secretly envied members of a clique you claimed to despise, did that make you a traitor? Iaian, who wasn't used to quandaries, found himself in one anyway. With Jemma being one of the enemy, Iaian didn't know how to behave. How could he show contempt for Andrew but kindness toward this amazing girl? How could his guys taunt the losers while leaving Jemma out of the mix? Jemma, who was aware of Iaian's crush, found her own hormonal power amusing. But Iaian was not amused.

For the first time, Iaian resented his clique. He bristled at the membership rules for a group that he himself had started. Was he falling in love with this girl—at least falling for his *idea* of her? Her dislike of him only increased his desire. Iaian had to make a choice: play the cartoon-character group leader or follow his heart and lose his friends. Being leader required him to be an a-hole; if the others saw how weak he was, they'd only attack him like hawks on a chicken. Iaian would never live it down. Like the Jewish friend who could not forgive his buddy's religious conversion, they'd view friendliness toward any member of Andrew's group as a betrayal of faith, a poke in the eye.

Not knowing where he belonged, Iaian became more introspective, and his change in demeanor was noticeable. Iaian could no longer muster the energy to incite contempt or conflict. His friends were itchy to make some trouble, but Iaian's sudden slackness sapped the energy from the group. Soon enough, his two main guys went their own way with a Tea Party thug. Four of the others stayed friends with Iaian, but now, sometimes, he actually found himself alone— unthinkable in his junior year. He would watch Andrew's peaceful group from a distance, with Jemma laughing alongside them.

For her part, Jemma noticed this different Iaian; solitude had made him more interesting. He wasn't Ellen DeGeneres, but now that Iaian had taken to wearing T-shirts to class instead of Brooks Brothers blazers, Jemma thought he was pretty sweet. When Iaian finally mustered the courage to introduce himself—his heart pounding out of his chest—Jemma's friendliness surprised him. She was pleasantly surprised by how shy Iaian was without his cronies. Gone were the macho posturing, the showing off, the better-than-you-ness. Standing outside their physics class, with none of their friends around to judge them, Iaian and Jemma talked to each other for the first time. Their circles didn't match, but they might.

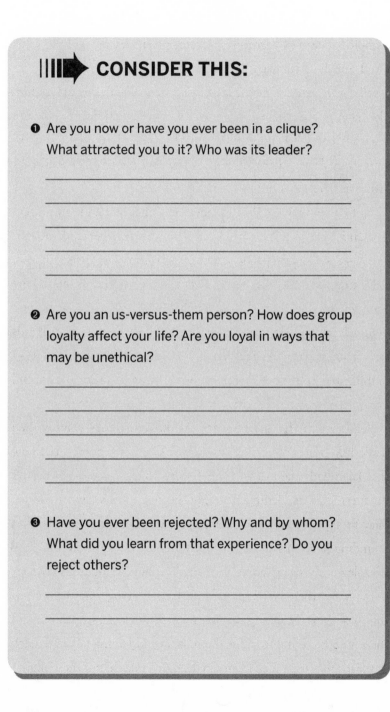

CONSIDER THIS:

❶ Are you now or have you ever been in a clique?
   What attracted you to it? Who was its leader?

_____

_____

_____

_____

_____

❷ Are you an us-versus-them person? How does group
   loyalty affect your life? Are you loyal in ways that
   may be unethical?

_____

_____

_____

_____

_____

❸ Have you ever been rejected? Why and by whom?
   What did you learn from that experience? Do you
   reject others?

_____

_____

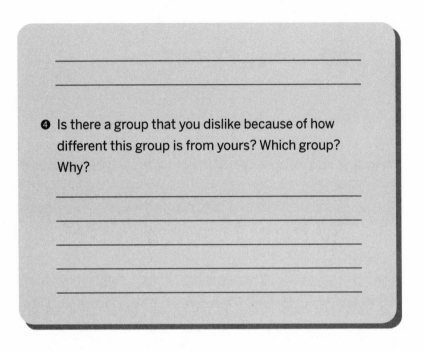

❹ Is there a group that you dislike because of how
different this group is from yours? Which group?
Why?

FOURTEEN

When Friends Lie

Beth had known Christopher a long time before she realized that he was a liar. Not a fibber. Not an occasional truth stretcher. Not a change-the-facts-to-spare-someone's-feelings-once-in-a-while fabricator. But a conscience-free, habitual liar who used misinformation and glaring omission to shape his image in the world and get ahead with his tall tales.

Beth was not a gullible person—but she was idealistic about honesty between friends. She'd been raised to believe that friendship was a sacred contract between people guaranteeing truth and transparency. Beth assumed that such candor was something respected by all friends. This is how assumptions trap us and outfit us with ethical blinders. Assumptions about friends can blind us to facts. Assumptions are "heuristic devices," emotional shorthand, that invite us to stop observing closely or take in information contradictory to what we already know (stereotyping serves the same social function). It's impossible to live without assumptions about our friends—imagine having to reappraise every friendship with each new encounter—but these assumptions come with built-in blind spots, as Beth came to realize with Christopher.

Her wake-up began with Christopher's lie about his father's funeral. Christopher was voluntarily estranged from his family, whom he blamed for everything wrong with his life, although he was almost forty. Like many neurotics engaged in perennial therapy, Christopher blamed his present on his past. He'd invented a self-excusing mythology around parental neglect that he suffered as a child. Christopher's parents were the villains of this myth wherein he was unloved, unseen, and misunderstood. He had incorporated this myth of childhood neglect as an excuse for all of his personal failings and banished his parents from his life as a way of keeping this fiction alive. Then Christopher's father died.

As it happened, Beth and Christopher were watching TV at his house when the call came from his mother. "Chris," an old lady's voice said on the message machine, "Daddy's gone. Please call me back. I hope that you can come down for the funeral." Beth was surprised by the affection in Christopher's mother's voice. She sounded nothing like the sadistic monster he had made her out to be. "Please call me back. I miss you, Chris. It's Mama."

Christopher ignored the call and did not attend his father's funeral. Although Beth was confused by this decision, she knew better than to lecture him on the subject of filial piety. When Christopher explained to Beth that his mother's call had been nothing but a ruse—that she didn't *really* want him to come— Beth did her best to believe this far-fetched story. Families are mysterious systems whose codes and signs are hard to decipher when you're inside them; from the outside, it's next to impossible to know for sure *what* is going on. Beth convinced herself that Christopher was telling the truth and attempted to mind her own business. Then the revealing lie was spoken and she realized that her friend was a faker. They were having dinner with their friend Larry a few weeks after Christopher's father's death. Larry offered his condolences, which Christopher brushed off like so much cat hair. "It's still sad to lose a parent," said Larry.

"Not when they don't love you," said Christopher.

Beth bit her tongue. "How do you know that?" Larry asked. "Some people have a hard time showing it."

"How about the fact that I wasn't invited to the funeral?" Christopher said.

"You're kidding!" Larry exclaimed.

"Would I kid about a thing like that?" asked Christopher, glaring at Beth as if daring her to mention his mother's voice-mail message. "You don't think that hurts?"

"That's rough," said Larry.

"I'm used to it," said Christopher. "It's par for the course."

Beth avoided looking at Christopher and finished her meal in a hurry. At home, she felt tormented by her friend's self-serving, bald-faced lie. How could Christopher have said that? In front of her! Had he no shame? She was unexpectedly outraged and angry. Something about it being a lie regarding the death of his own father, a thing that Beth considered sacred, made it especially odious. Beth thought about his mother's kind voice, and Christopher's self-victimizing charade, and became even more angry. She doubted whether she could be Christopher's friend without confronting him. The disgust that Beth felt was so profound, even she could not understand it.

Disgust is the foundation of all moral choice, it is interesting to learn. The origins of how disgust evolved as a moral emotion are mind-blowing, too, as I reported in *Ethical Wisdom*. As meat eaters, humans developed extra sensitivity to disgust as a way of not contaminating ourselves. (We are one of only four omnivorous species—the others are herring gulls, cockroaches, and vultures.) Disgust—the gag reflex—enabled us to forage through the world without poisoning ourselves. As a moral emotion, it does much the same. Disgust helps to protect our character from corruptive forces in the environment. An emotion that originates in putrefaction results in its own kind of gag reflex that signifies much more than microbe avoidance. Over time, disgust became the guardian of human virtue, deeply tied to sacredness. For the Hopi, the word for disgust is synonymous with "world out of balance."

Beth's world was out of balance indeed after realizing that Christopher was such a liar. Lying between friends is especially outrageous. Dishonesty tends to cause moral offense in proportion to how close people are to us. We do not respond to strangers' lies with the same vehemence we do to lies told by friends and family. Studies show that lying and cheating increase, as you might expect, in proportion to the unlikelihood of parties meeting again. We modulate our ethical choices to match the threat of consequences. The lower the probability of getting caught, the more likely we are to be dishonest. In less than intimate contexts such as business, for instance, we permit omissions and truth stretching that would be considered shameful with friends or family. If we treated our friends as deceptively as we do strangers and rivals, it's unlikely that they would stay our friends.

It is naïve to imagine that lying is always wrong, however. We Americans, bred from Puritans, have a uniquely judgmental attitude to lying not shared by other cultures. I asked an Englishwoman in my study group how she felt about lying to friends. She laughed. "Very friendly." She could not imagine telling the truth all the time. Though kindhearted, she claimed this would be a disaster. The Englishwoman gave the example of a newly widowed friend with a terrible face-lift. "Should I tell her she looks like a mummy?" she asked. "Of course not. That is not what friends do. When the damage cannot be undone, and it is not life threatening, friends lie. I consider it an act of friendship to offer hope, not brutality. Had she asked my advice before having the surgery, I would have advised her to focus on her inner beauty. But she did not. To be honest with her now would to be to punish her with the truth—more for my sake than hers. That is not how friends behave."

Being unconstructively truthful is worse than lying to give a friend courage. That is why we call them white lies. White lies do no harm. They carry no great consequence and call for no great fabrication. The lies we tell to help our friends (not habitually, but now and then) are part and parcel of intimacy. Intimacy is the adaptive behavior of imperfect beings in an imperfect world. By definition, intimacy is imperfect, too, which is why when a beloved elderly friend asks if she looks pretty enough to go out on a date, you tell her, yes, she does absolutely, and that any guy would be lucky to have her (*with or without a perfect face-lift*, you think). We do not bludgeon our friends with the truth because this is not how love behaves. Truth telling can be selfish and more harmful than a white lie told with good intentions. Though Puritans rail against ethical subtlety and refuse any exception to being 100 percent honest, they risk inflicting harm when it is not necessary.

Obviously, lying to friends is a last resort and not a way of life. People like Christopher who find it easier to lie than bear the discomfort of truthfulness cannot be trusted until they come clean, regardless of our affection for them. Beth needed Christopher to come clean. Being truthful with herself about Christopher, she was forced to admit that he'd always been a little shady and this had always bugged her. There was an unevenness, a characteristic imbalance, in their friendship that had always been there. Globetrotting Christopher and loyal Beth. She was tired of the cat-and-mouse game. Beth was forced to admit to herself that she did not even like Christopher, not as much as she pretended to. There was something missing in him, and this missing chip prevented emotional traction, the groove that true friends can fall into together, when they don't have to think about it. Beth linked this emotional gap to a hollowness in Christopher's character, the way he preened and posed and postured in the reflecting pool of the world's eyes. After all these years, Beth acknowledged her own ambivalence and wondered what this self-deception said about *her*? What other untruths had she kept to herself? How honest was Beth, really?

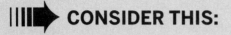 **CONSIDER THIS:**

❶ How often do you lie to friends? What motivates you to lie? Do you feel guilty for the lies you tell?

_____

_____

_____

_____

_____

❷ Do you expect friends to be completely truthful with you at all times? If not, when? And why not?

_____

_____

_____

_____

_____

❸ How do you define a white lie? Is it wrong to tell white lies? Have you ever been hurt by a white lie?

_____

_____

_____

_____

_____

❹ Have you ever felt moral disgust toward a friend? Was this disgust deserved? If so, why? If not, why not?

_____

_____

_____

_____

_____

FIFTEEN

The Fragility
of Trust

Trust in friendship is more fragile than we like to acknowledge. Until you have lost an old friend, you will not have learned this important lesson. Here are the two most frequently forgotten wisdom lessons in friendship: First, friendship must be *earned* and maintained; second, trust is paper thin and, once punctured, difficult if not impossible to repair just as good as new.

The terror of losing our closest friends is too close for comfort to be acknowledged. We adapt to this insecurity by living as if our friends belonged to us, somehow (just like our lives), as if they were *ours* for the duration, barring mayhem, murder, or major deceit. In the same way that we take existence for granted, we take the liberty of ignoring our dearest friends with the assumption that these dear ones will wait in the wings for us while the romance, new job, baby, or crisis passes. We trust too much in the illusion of forevermore, and this hubris makes us bad friends. It can also make us betray one another in ways we may not comprehend.

I know a woman who takes her friends for granted. She strings them along like the Pied Piper of canceled appointments. She is one of the greatest seducers I know. Her MO goes something like this: First, she lures newcomers into her life with generosity stemming from low self-esteem, magnanimity based on hating herself and needing people around to adore her. Once they're hooked, she distances herself from these very friends because she cannot stand to be pawed at. Though impromptu fondness comes naturally, intimacy is a problem for her. You never quite know where you stand with her, how much of her affection is sincere and how much of it is politeness and needing people to think she's a saint.

I have a hard time trusting her. I like her a lot and could imagine being more personal. But that would require knowing that she would not disappear. This trust handicap is easy to explain: This friend will never initiate contact. She will never, under any circumstances, pick up the phone first or reveal that she actually wants to see you. When pressed, she will tell you that she's too insecure, too scared of rejection to be proactive, but this excuse will not stand. All of us are forced to go out on a limb for love, to risk looking foolish, or smitten, or needy, in the crooked act of caring for others, whether the love is platonic or not. It's not ethical to cry *scared* and expect to be trusted. This fear prevents friends from becoming too personal. I could not trust this woman because she remained *impersonal*. That was the word I could find to describe it. She never really dropped her mask. She lacked the courage to show her need.

This created a frustrating bond. Every few months, after she'd canceled at least once, we'd have a great evening and promise to see each other more often, knowing that unless I pursued her, this would never happen. Trust would not grow in this one-way arrangement. Personal friendship means mutual action. Friendship does truly need to be earned. A person needs to drop the mask in order to earn the trust of another. Our brains are wired to detect insincerity. A two-year-old baby can differentiate between sincerity and impersonal treatment. Different parts of the brain light up in personal versus impersonal encounters.

Philosopher Martin Buber had a brilliant way of articulating this trust gap in the brain. He described *I-You* versus *I-It* relationships. In I-You relationships, we treat one another personally, heart to heart, without fear of the other's humanity. We do this because we seek connection, and because we feel empathy for one another (*not* pity, which is an I-It thing). I-You relationships bring us closer by forcing us to drop the impersonal mask and revealing our own all-too-human flaws. Generosity arising from I-You connection creates trust, because we can feel that it is intended for us; it is not generic. By definition, I-You relationships are reciprocal.

I-It connections are completely different. I-It relationships
are not the meetings of equals, but interactions based on need
wherein one party is the consumer, the other the consumed. If
you saw the film *The Devil Wears Prada*, you witnessed Meryl
Streep as the imperious bitch goddess/fashion editrix treating the
immediate world in the royal I-It. We all have both kinds of relationships. When you speak to a bank clerk, are you talking to a
person or a set of hands with money? Do you care what this person has to say? Or do you treat what comes out of their mouth as
superfluous information, and would you mind just giving me my
withdrawal, please?

I-It relationships preclude trust and undermine feelings of self-
worth. A fireman from Texas wrote me this letter after reading
Ethical Wisdom:

> Barry and I spent twelve years on the same ladder
> at our station house. He was a little guy, barely five feet
> tall. All of us treated him like the station mascot, me the
> worst of all. We turned him into our little servant. Sweetest
> guy you ever met. Always the first to volunteer. But some-
> thing about him—or about us—I wouldn't say we bullied him,
> but we just didn't really appreciate him, except as a go-
> fer. We bossed him around like he was our lackey. I see it
> now in retrospect. Barry never complained. Then, one day,
> he just up and quit. He never said a word to us. Barry
> said good-bye to the chief and told him he was sick of
> being taken for granted. Nobody gave him any respect.
> We felt bad afterward but it was too late.

To his colleagues at the firehouse, Barry was an *it*, not a *you*. Lack of respect drove Barry away. He did not trust that he truly mattered. I understood how this might feel; in a different way, I felt it with my hard-to-get friend. But she and I had an empathy breakthrough. After not seeing her for months, I called but she did not phone me back. A distant friendship went suddenly silent. I wasn't even completely surprised—I never really trusted her. Then curiosity got the better of me and I wrote her a letter to ask what had happened. I like to get the information, at least, and learn if possible from what has happened, so that lousy things serve some benefit. With this woman, I had nothing to lose. Worst scenario, she would freeze me out, which she was doing anyway. At least I'd know I had made the effort.

What happened next came as a big surprise. This friend called and thanked me profusely for writing. She knew that the note had come at a cost, and my effort caused her to pick up the phone at last. The following day, we met for coffee. From the moment she entered the restaurant, I could see that something had changed in her. When she saw me, her smile was finally sincere. She touched my hand and told me she was glad to see me. I asked her what had happened.

She swallowed hard and her eyes teared up. She looked more tender and exposed than I'd ever seen her. "I feel so stupid," she said. "Like junior high."

"Life is junior high," I told her.

Without meaning to, I had hurt her feelings. Not thinking she cared, I'd assembled a dinner party of mutual friends without inviting her. As she'd never included me in her intimate sphere (I always felt second-tier), it had not occurred to me to include her. Incredibly enough, this oversight was upsetting enough to her that she could not bring herself to speak to me. Finally, I saw that our friendship mattered precisely because that had caused her pain. Hearts are often revealed sideways like this, inadvertently. When I saw the emotion in her face, I trusted her for the first time.

Naturally, as Beth learned over Christopher's lie (in the last chapter), we must trust one another factually. But factual lying and emotional lying are not unrelated. In the same way that Beth could not connect to Christopher through his dissimulation, I had been incapable of connecting fully with this lady through the veil of feigned apathy.

Now, when she's chilly or distant or completely absent, I have this memory of her mask slipping off to fall back on. I still have my doubts about what makes her tick—distant people are a mystery to me. I still wish she'd be the first one to pick up the phone or initiate a date. But now I can give her the benefit of the doubt because we have established a personal connection. In the candor required to clear up what happened, we went from I-It to I-You, and that made all the difference.

▐▐▐▶ CONSIDER THIS:

❶ Who do you take for granted in your life?

_____

_____

_____

_____

_____

❷ What steps can you take to be more demonstrative?

_____

_____

_____

_____

_____

❸ When and with whom are you insincere in your affections?

_____

_____

_____

_____

_____

❹ Does trust come hard to you? Why? Or are you too trusting?

_____

_____

_____

_____

_____

❺ Is loyalty a high value to you? What does loyalty mean in your friendships?

_____

_____

_____

_____

_____

SIXTEEN

The Mate You Can't Stand

D arlene was a bitch—and Daniel wasn't the only one to
think so. Darlene was married to Craig, Daniel's best
friend and his partner at a stress-reduction clinic in San
Diego. Darlene, who called herself an artist, was a woman who
looked down on everyone around her (picture a duchess scowl-
ing at peasants), expecting her whims to be catered to. Few could
bear Darlene's condescension but Daniel absolutely detested her.
To begin with, he knew that Darlene was a fraud as an artist. Her
specialty was religious sculpture splattered with epoxy to look like

bird poop), overpriced pieces of ugly kitsch—*Jesus After Pigeons,
Buddha After Pigeons*—as ugly as they were laughable. Like many
frauds, Darlene believed that she was a genius, and this pretense
combined with her snottiness made Daniel extremely angry. Just
the sight of Darlene, willowy, wan, and self-aggrandizing, gripped
Daniel's entrails with fury.

When Daniel went into business with Craig, he knew that
Darlene was part of the package. Still, Daniel imagined that Darlene would do *something* to ingratiate herself to him and his wife,
Rose, who couldn't stand her either. But this something had never
happened. With each career disappointment, midlife crisis, Botox
resmoothing, and medication adjustment, Darlene only grew
more poisonous. Craig was blind to his wife's flaws, amazingly,
and worshipped the ground she spat on. Trapped in a Gordian
knot of aversion, Daniel, a diplomat by nature, forced himself
to become the picture of politeness on those rare, dreaded occasions when he could not avoid having face time with Darlene. But
even Daniel had his limits.

The night things turned ugly, Rose and Daniel had agreed to
meet Craig and Darlene for a pre-Christmas dinner at Fondue
Heaven. "Who the hell eats fondue?" asked Rose on the way to
the restaurant. Darlene had insisted on the venue and would not
brook negotiation. On arrival, they found Craig and a miserable-
looking Darlene waiting for them in a corner booth. Rose and
Daniel tried to make small talk, but Darlene refused to say a
word; she was too busy texting, complaining under her breath,
and emptying the bottle of wine. The food came and Craig made

a valiant attempt to cheer her up, while Daniel and Rose helped themselves to the heart attack in a Crock-Pot. "Isn't she something else?" he asked, rhetorically, stroking Darlene's hair. "I'm a pretty lucky guy."

Darlene batted his hand away and went back to her smart phone. Attempting to out-bitch, Rose pretended to take her side. "Leave her alone," she said. "We girls need to be alone with our thoughts sometimes. Don't we, doll?"

Darlene leered at Rose like something stuck to her shoe. "I beg your pardon?"

"I was just—"

"I heard you," Darlene said, stabbing at the fondue with a triangle of toast. "You think I need you to talk for me?"

Rose's mouth twitched in a way that warned Daniel that she was about to blow. "Can't tell when you're being patronized, honey?"

"Honey? *You* are patronizing *me*?"

Rose laughed and muttered under her breath, "It's not exactly hard."

"You? Who vacuum for a living?"

Rose's mouth twitched. She was three times smarter than Darlene and could have laid her out cold with a single punch (which she would have gladly delivered). Instead, she lowered her voice to an acid whisper. "You're absolutely right, Darlene. Instead of taking care of my family, I could be making shitty art that nobody buys and pretending like I'm Picasso. What was I thinking?"

"Now, Rose—" Daniel tried to run interference.

"How dare you," Darlene said.

"That was uncalled for," Craig added.

"No," said Rose. "It really wasn't."

Darlene stood up, threw down her napkin, and stomped out of Fondue Heaven with her tie-dye culottes in a twist. Craig, who appeared not to know what to do, asked Rose if that was necessary. "Damn straight," Rose replied. "That was cumulative," Daniel added. "So much for friends," Craig said, nonsensically. Then he slapped a hundred-buck bill on the table, wished Daniel and Rose a merry Christmas, and followed his wife out the door.

Wonderful people have terrible spouses. Sweet-natured people align with some pigs. What's a friend to do, though, with a sow like Darlene, the marital baggage that comes with a buddy? Is it possible to be friends with someone and hide how you feel about their significant other? Or is friendship with people with intolerable spouses necessarily doomed from the start? Can friends with ill-fitting partners maintain their relationships separately? Or do coupled people come in pairs—take them or leave them—and best not to try to tell ourselves anything different?

For starters, it helps to remember that kin selection is serious business (as we learned when dealing with other people's children). Loyalty to family, including mates, always supersedes loyalty to friends. If something comes between you and a friend's spouse, you are the one who will be eighty-sixed. Enmity between you and a friend's partner automatically puts you at risk; when you conspire with friends against their spouses (or concur too wholeheartedly with their complaints), you will be held accountable when they make up. Instead, it is advisable to ingratiate yourself whenever possible to spouses you can't stand, to be extra friendly, extra accommodating, and appear extra pleased to see them. This is false, in the sense of not being true, but true in the sense of being wise. Your extra effort to get over yourself will make you a better person and protect your friend from having to dump you when you cannot get along with their partner.

Being kind to individuals we do not like is a form of spiritual practice. Honoring the person beloved by a friend is another way of loving them. Mary discovered this with Yuval, the fiancée of her dear friend Kendra. Mary, an ardent feminist, had a hard time accepting this macho man whom Kendra was about to marry. Yuval had been in the Israeli army; there are few men more brave, though arrogant, than an Israeli soldier. His very rectitude made Mary's Gloria Steinem back go up like a cat's. Yuval was also flirtatious toward women, adding an extra sexual edge to an already irritated feminist dynamic that strained Mary's friendship with Kendra to the limit. Then Mary saw what she was doing—what she was about to do—and made a spiritual decision. She decided to hold nothing against Yuval, to the best of her ability, to let him start with a fresh slate. To help her do this, Mary began what I call the One Good Thing practice. She determined to find one thing about Yuval that she could not *not* respect. This would put her in an ethical checkmate and force Mary to let down her guard. Yuval had rescued a shelter animal, a beat-up old shepherd he named Rex, with hip dysplasia, a wonky eye, and a battered coat that was burned in parts where his owner had played a game with matches and lighter fluid.

Mary's heart went out to Rex, who'd been spared euthanasia by Yuval's kindness alone. Thinking about his kindness made Mary feel kinder. She stroked Rex's belly and watched Yuval knead Kendra's shoulders and felt the love between them. It's harder to hate a person who's making someone you love so happy. Mary felt her disgust fade slowly, averting the inevitable collision with Yuval that would have robbed her of a friend. This is how friendship teaches skillful means, mindfulness, self-transcendence, even wisdom when we have no choice but to care for someone we dislike as a way of preserving what we treasure.

Spiritual practice is all about working "against the grain," as Buddhists say. We work against our own smallness, judgments, and controlling nature. Instead of tightening our opinions, we expand them, and one excellent way of doing this is with people we are stuck with. Disliked partners of people we love are people we are stuck with. Like family, they force our hand. Another tenet of spiritual practice is that we tend not to do it until we have to. Yuval forced Mary's spiritual hand. She would have to get over her politics in order to respond from her highest self. The same could not be said of Darlene, who carried the grudge against Rose's insult till the day she died. That night at Fondue Heaven was the last dinner the couples ate together. Craig and Daniel no longer socialized; six months later, Craig bought Daniel out and he took Rose back to New Jersey, where they were from, leaving Craig and Darlene—who refused to speak to them—back on the West Coast. Darlene's work has still not found its market. She blames the market, but really it's because the stuff's not attractive. Who wants a Buddha head covered in bird poop? Daniel and Rose could never quite figure.

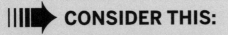 **CONSIDER THIS:**

❶ How do you behave toward the spouse or partner
you don't like? What are your specific criticisms of
this person? Are they justified?

_____

_____

_____

_____

_____

❷ How do you behave when your friends dislike your
spouse or partner? Are you defensive? Do you take
sides? Are they justified?

_____

_____

_____

_____

_____

❸ Do you believe that coupled friends can or should
have individual friendships? Or is a couple obliged to
socialize together? Is it rude to invite one without
the other? Why?

_____

❹ When was the last time you made a conscious effort to move beyond your own opinions about a friend's spouse or partner? Did you succeed? How did that feel?

SEVENTEEN

One Up, One Down

Power is catnip to human beings. It begins in our family constellations, where dominance and submission come into play the moment we're brought home from the hospital and placed in the crib. From there, we realize how small we are in comparison to our parents and siblings, giants who treat us inconsistently at best. As babies, we learn to manipulate; babies are expert manipulators. Studies show that human infant features evolved to be cute precisely in order to dominate the emotions of their parents. As children grow, this power play extends to our first friends, who help us to understand who we are and where we fall in the social pecking order. It's easy to spot dominant and submissive children on any playground. The alphas are calling the shots, the betas are telling them how cool they are, the omegas are trying to just fit in.

Mickey was a natural-born omega. Half the size of his classmates, the only son in a fatherless home ruled by a tyrannical mother, Mickey was born to be second banana, to serve, to please, to be chosen for the kickball team only if everyone else had already been chosen. Excessively sweet-natured, happiest when everyone he cared about, or wanted to please, had everything that they needed whether he did himself or not, Mickey was a natural acolyte, a follower of many leaders, a fetcher of sodas, a sweeper of floors, an excuser of other people's misdeeds, an apologist for those who hurt him ("They didn't mean it"), and the boy in his second-grade class most likely to grow up to be a doormat.

Alan was the class alpha. Also from a fatherless home, but one where the mother was mostly absent, Alan had a king-sized chip on his shoulder and refused to be told what to do or admit if he had made a mistake. When Alan wanted something he took it with or without permission. Alan hated authority. He could not, *would* not, submit, either to his teachers or to the other kids. Alan stomped his way around the playground like an eight-year-old Patton in beat-up sneakers his mother was too broke to replace and felt superior to everyone. That's what he told himself, at least, which helped because inside he felt like a freak.

Mickey admired Alan. He thought that Alan was cool. He admired the way Alan swaggered and sneered and imagined Alan protecting him at recess. One day, Mrs. Edelman, their teacher, returned a math quiz that Alan had flunked. Mickey had gotten an A-minus. Alan caught up with Mickey on the playground. "Hey, math mouse," Alan said. Mickey asked him if he needed some help. "What makes you think I need help, rodent?"

"Nobody needs to know," said Mickey.

"Why don't you just let me cheat?"

Mickey knew that this was wrong, but he said, "Okay."

"You promise to keep your mouth shut?" said Alan.

"I won't tell."

Alan was the master, Mickey the slave. Alan demanded and Mickey fulfilled. Alan put the fear of God into Mickey, threatening to tell his most painful secrets (sitting down when he peed, wearing a coat from the Salvation Army), while Mickey, in turn, was enslaved by shame and a dire need for Alan not to reject him. As with any grown-up masochist, abuse made Mickey all the more smitten. He confused Alan's need with affection. As with any grown-up sadist, power made Alan all the more bossy; Mickey's devotion, help, and loyalty were confused with a voice saying, "Kick me, please." What happened next would teach Mickey a lesson that served him for the rest of his life.

We play "one up, one down" games with friends quite often. We play different roles with different people, depending on temperament, timing, and need. We may be dominated by one friend's neuroses, another's needs, the superior intelligence of yet another. Without realizing it, we regularly expect friends to submit to us, as well, according to our mood or disposition. This is part of the natural give-and-take of needy, greedy, self-interested people on the roller coaster of their lives.

This is only a problem when we get stuck in a fixed, unhealthy power struggle. When friendship is monitored by a sense of fairness, with neither party hogging the driver's seat, power ought not to be a problem between friends. But friendship without parity is inauthentic. It's exploitation, usury, ego-tripping, and collusion, even when sub-dom relationships are full of affection. Just as romantic affairs based on lust or exploitation don't deserve to be called love (the French call them *arrangements*), friendships based on power (or a passing math grade) dissolve the moment the need is met or one party breaks the unspoken agreement to remain in his or her position. Mickey would find that out soon enough.

Ursula had another method for lording it over the friends in her life. As the mother of an autistic son, her days were spent scrambling between specialists' offices, special care schools, special meetings for parents like her, and the couch of a special therapist who told Ursula how amazing she was for raising a child as difficult as hers was. Ursula wore her maternal affliction loudly; her son was her hair shirt, her cross to bear; his condition had robbed her of freedom, as a single mother, and so Ursula took it out on her girlfriends. When plans were made, her needs came first; when plans were broken, it was always by her; when eating out with friends, she hogged the attention and expected someone else to pay, since she was hoeing such a hard row. She milked the pathos like a bloated cow and grew indignant when others tried to suggest that they, too, had hardships in life that deserved a little air time and attention.

Ursula dominated with guilt and self-pity, using her pain like a dungeon master to gag friends with her personal woes. When they tried to escape—by avoiding her or suggesting that her life could be worse—she shamed them with accusations ("Go ahead, look the other way!") and the worst accusation of all: "Be a fair-weather friend." So drunk was Ursula on self-pity that her friends began to disappear. Unlike a true friend losing friends, however, she missed the audience more than the people themselves. Ursula cared most about her role, as the dominant presence, so filling the empty spots left by disappearing friends wasn't really *that* hard. Any shoulder to cry on would do, really, so long as the new friend was willing to wear the emotional handcuffs and didn't question who called the shots.

It's important to understand how roles work if we want to understand power in friendship. The most common power prize in friendship is who is getting more attention. Being paid attention to is a form of power, as the baby learned in the crib. We dominate by receiving care in the basest, most infantile ways, and, as friends, we understand this and sense whose need is greatest at any given moment. Aside from attention, we use other measurements of power in friendship. Grudges held, secrets kept, needs unmet, calls unanswered, promises not honored, loyalty ungiven, or wounds being licked in the form of withdrawal, silence, or ungenerosity may point to emotional power being wielded in unhelpful ways. In long-term friendships, emotional wounds may ossify over time into preconceptions about your friends, a way of viewing them that is filled with expectations that prevent you from seeing them as they are.

Mickey found out the hard way with Alan. Mrs. Edelman caught Alan looking at Mickey's test and hauled him out of class and to the VP's office. On his way out, Alan banged on Mickey's desk, and shouted, "Stop trying to show me your stupid test!" Alan never talked to Mickey again. Not a word. Mickey was inconsolable.

One day, after being kicked by a group of boys, he escaped recess and went to the school guidance counselor. Mickey was crying, and this kind young woman (she wasn't much older than his sister) took him into her office without an appointment and made Mickey tell her what had happened. She listened to the story about Alan and asked Mickey a question that sliced him open like a knife. "Why would you want someone like that to protect you?" Mickey didn't know what to say. He wanted to take care of himself, he thought for the first time. Mickey had never stood up for himself in the slightest. It had never seemed a possibility; he'd get punished at home for not obeying. But why was he obeying Alan? He knew that cheating was wrong. He also knew it wasn't his idea.

Mickey then made the change that would stick—a change that would later change his life. He opened his mouth and told the truth. First, Mickey told the truth to the girls in class—that Alan had come to him—knowing it would travel fast. Alan responded to this insurrection with a backhand slap across Mickey's face during recess, which, in turn, brought the five most popular girls in class running, while Alan sulked under a tree and looked like a bully. The girls asked Mickey if he was okay. "I'll never be a jerk like that," he told them. In Mickey's eyes, Alan looked smaller, all by himself on the grass in the shade. The girls let Mickey eat lunch at their table.

CONSIDER THIS:

❶ Do you ever dominate your friends?
How? Why? When?

_____
_____
_____
_____
_____

❷ Is it important for you to feel liked? What will you
do to create this feeling with friends?

_____
_____
_____
_____
_____

❸ Are you aware of power in friendships?
Is this something that attracts or repels you?
Why, truthfully?

_____
_____
_____

_____

_____

❹ Is there a hierarchy in your circle of friends?
Where do you stand? How do you feel about this?

_____

_____

_____

_____

_____

EIGHTEEN

Friends in Need

Hannah avoided hip replacement surgery for years till the pain became unbearable. Although Hannah was only forty-two, decades as a professional dancer had left her in chronic pain, unable to enjoy many of the things (shopping, aerobics, sex) a woman her age still wants to enjoy. Hannah dreaded the operation and six-week recovery time but was more afraid of not being able to walk, so she gathered her courage and set the date.

Her best friend, Calvin, was scared, too, but for different reasons. Calvin had a new man in his life and was terrified of getting dumped. Flamboyant, self-absorbed, and domineering, Calvin—who'd been Hannah's partner in the dance company—was her dearest, most reliable friend except when there was a boyfriend around. Then Calvin ignored everything and everyone other than the object of his affection. He'd disappear for weeks on end till the romance fizzled—they always fizzled—then come back to Hannah, heartbroken, tail between his legs. She was always happy to take him back because Calvin was a wonderful friend and so unlike the other men in her life, the ones Hannah dated, who tended to be successful but emotionally distant.

Calvin's current obsession was a dentist named Neil who was ten years younger and driving him crazy. When Hannah called to tell Calvin about the surgery, he was in a tizzy. Neil hadn't called *all day*. Calvin was sure he had disappeared. "I'm too old to be single," Calvin moaned. "I can't go through this again!"

"I know," Hannah said. "Breathe." This is what she always told Calvin when he was hyperventilating. "Meanwhile, I've got some good news."

"Why doesn't he call?"

"I'm having the surgery. I will need you."

"The what?"

"My hips."

"What about them?"

Hannah winced. They'd been commiserating over their dance-ravaged hips for a decade, twisted up from too many ballet extensions. Their battle scars were something that they had in common, a survivor's cross they hoisted together. Hannah said, "I set the date."

"For your hips?" Calvin asked, still distracted.

"Helloooo!"

"Oh, good for you." Calvin could not have sounded less supportive. "Not a great time for me, though."

"Not a good time?" Hannah was starting to bristle.

"I'll do what I can. I mean, of *course*." Hannah could hear the subtext underneath his half-hearted promise ("Not now. Please. This could be Mr. Right").

"You sure you wouldn't rather wait?" Calvin asked.

"It hurts when I walk," Hannah reminded him. Calvin made no reply. Before screaming at him, or starting to cry, Hannah hung up the phone. She felt wounded by Calvin's apathy. Hannah had always told herself that if push came to shove, she always had Calvin, that friendships like theirs always came first. Her belief in their friendship made Hannah feel safe and less alone in the world. With the surgery looming, she felt more alone than usual and waited for Calvin to show up. She waited for a message assuring her that he would be there hook, line, and sinker. But all she received were text messages that left her more upset than before. Hannah decided to ignore Calvin. In the days leading up to the surgery, she did not call or rely upon Calvin and accepted her sister's help instead. Though she had announced the big day on Facebook, numerous times, and Calvin must know it was coming, he did not contact her. Not till she was in pre-op did her sister tell Hannah that Calvin had left a message, wishing her luck, and saying how swell things were going with Neil.

Hannah could not forgive him. The operation went smoothly, but afterward she did not return Calvin's texts or phone calls.

She felt like a woman scorned, and the combination of physical weakness, anger, and neediness took Hannah into a depression. She had not realized quite how much she had come to rely on Calvin. Not merely the flesh-and-blood Calvin but the *idea* of him. The idea that someone was standing beside her, confirming that Hannah had a backup (family excluded) in case of emergency. Never before had Hannah realized just how alone she felt. Flat on her back with an ice pack beneath her hips, she watched as her sister fetched and carried (without complaint for a change), contemplating this depression, reaching down into it like a bog, the swamp of her own loneliness. In the middle of this loneliness, Hannah sensed a rock—a solid grudge of need—that she carried without knowing it. This rock was labeled SELF-PITY, something Hannah had never truly acknowledged (and might not have if Calvin had not deserted her).

As Hannah lay there recuperating, she came to realize, reluctantly, that although her friend had disappointed her, his letdown wasn't the major point here. She was not depressed because of Calvin. Hannah was depressed, she understood, because she was tired of being alone, tired of her noncommittal dates, tired of her obsessive gay friend, and tired, she came to sob into her pillow, *of her life*. She stopped wanting badly for Calvin to call—needing him to call—aware of an even deeper yearning for a different kind of a life, a whole new kind of connection, a partner she could actually count on, a man who was in it for real.

When Calvin called the next time, Hannah wasn't even hurt anymore, and when he came by a week later with Neil, who seemed perfectly nice, she was able to be friendly and gracious. But her friendship with Calvin had changed for good. Hannah's trust was torn to shreds. And she no longer needed the idea of Calvin. In a short time, they had outgrown one another, left twenty years of entwinement behind them. Now that Calvin had a man—at least for the moment—and Hannah had a new pair of hips on which to stride, it was time for both of them to move on. If Calvin's relationship fell apart, he'd know better than to run back to Hannah, expecting her to coddle him. She could be his friend but not his security blanket, just as Calvin could no longer keep his thumb in the dike between Hannah and loneliness. That was the job of another man if she could ever find him.

Friends in need are a tricky equation. Friends are bound to us by choice, not obligation. Unlike needy family members, needy friends can be ignored with a certain impunity. Of course, we help friends when possible and do our best to keep promises, hoping for the same care from them. But friends are not family when the chips are down, and we are wise to know this. For example, two of my closest male friends are married with kids. Although we are devoted friends and can count on each other for many things, let a wife or child require something and my needs disappear from view, which is exactly as it should be. Such prioritizing is in the natural order. Expecting our needs to be met by friends is childish. Projecting infantile needs on friendship, we suffocate them. If friendships are not to become incestuous stand-ins for family love, they fare better with clarity, boundaries,

and space—rather than fantasized obligation—as Hannah's disil-
lusionment taught her.

Being voluntary, help in friendship is also more selfless than
kin selection, and closer to altruism (our genes don't benefit from
helping friends). Altruism is the self-transcending emotion that
prompts us to help for the sake of helping, or because helping
increases the strength of the community. When friends help
friends it's more heroic because they don't stand to benefit.

Yelena learned this unexpectedly when she was about to lose
her home. An unemployed nurse in a default-happy community,
where property values were lower than mortgages, Yelena had
reached the end of her rope. She was nearly three months behind
on her house payment. Yelena's parents could not help her, and
her pride would not allow her to ask friends for help. In the former Soviet Union, where Yelena was born, self-reliance was next
to godliness, prompted partly by a distrust of human nature, after
so many years under Communist rule. Her parents taught Yelena
and her siblings that family only could be counted upon because
"everyone else was out for themselves."

When Yelena's neighbor and friend, Ondrea, unexpectedly
offered to pay her mortgage, Yelena was flabbergasted. This spontaneous gesture of generosity contradicted what Yelena believed
about human nature. Altruism, which she had never believed in,
spontaneous, unmanipulative goodness did actually exist in the
world. This heartwarming knowledge changed Yelena and what
she believed was possible. A healing took place when she over-
came her shame and accepted Ondrea's loan. After that, Yelena

felt closer to Ondrea than to any friend she'd ever known, not only because she was helped but because Yelena realized that, in her friend's position, she would have done the same thing.

As for Hannah, her story ends happily, too. Two months after her surgery, Hannah showed up at the Friday night salsa class her girlfriends had been telling her about for years. For the first time in over a decade, Hannah danced pain free, miraculously, in high heels. Dancing seemed to give her her life back, and, with every lesson Hannah took, her confidence grew and she felt younger. When Calvin finally did get dumped, he left a text on Hannah's phone: *Maybe I deserved this one. Maybe he did,* Hannah thought, knowing she could not take Calvin back the way she used to. Instead, she sent Calvin a few words from Rilke, describing how love can feel when people actually trust one another, allowing each other the space to breathe. "Love consists in this, that two solitudes protect and touch and greet each other." Hannah typed these words into her phone and wondered if she'd ever meet a man who protected, touched, and greeted her, from his separate solitude. She wondered if Calvin would meet one, too, and what, if anything, he might have learned from their separation. Hannah needed nothing from him. This absence of clinging felt like love.

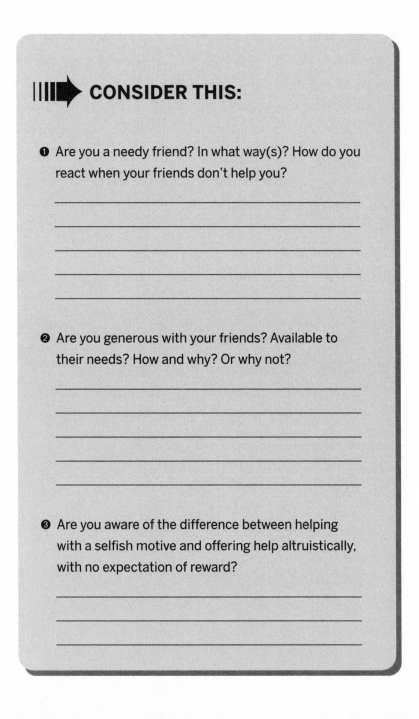

CONSIDER THIS:

❶ Are you a needy friend? In what way(s)? How do you react when your friends don't help you?

_____

_____

_____

_____

_____

❷ Are you generous with your friends? Available to their needs? How and why? Or why not?

_____

_____

_____

_____

_____

❸ Are you aware of the difference between helping with a selfish motive and offering help altruistically, with no expectation of reward?

_____

_____

_____

_____

_____

❹ What is the greatest favor that a friend ever did for
you? Did this act of generosity change your view
of human nature? If so, how? Was this shift in
perspective permanent?

_____

_____

_____

_____

_____

NINETEEN

When Friends Need to Intervene

I t is difficult to know in friendship when attempts should be made to intervene in cases where people are endangering their own lives.

Chris's weight was out of control. In the two years since Chris had been fired from his tree-trimming job in rural Vermont, he'd ballooned to nearly 400 pounds, leaving his friends at a loss about the right thing to do. They were divided up the middle, more or less, between the friends who thought it was none of their business, most of whom were men, and the friends who insisted that *someone* say something, as long as it wasn't them (most of these were women). They were worried about his heavy drinking, foul eating habits, and vicious self-recrimination, too, not to mention the agoraphobia that was getting worse as Chris got fatter and fatter, refusing to leave his apartment.

This downward spiral hit bottom on Saint Patrick's Day. For as long as Chris's friends could remember, he and the gang had celebrated Saint Paddy's in leprechaun hats at their favorite dive bar in Montpelier. Chris lived for Saint Paddy's Day with Ginny, Paul, Myrna, Lucy, Frank, and Pearl—his posse—and was as loyal as he was an alcoholic. Ever since high school, Chris had been the life of the party, the generous one you could count on day or night. If your car got stuck in the snow, you called Chris not the Triple-A. If you needed a couple of bucks for rent, Chris wrote you a check with no questions asked. If your girlfriend or boyfriend dumped you, it was Chris who made sure you had something to do on a Friday night, and Chris who remembered your birthday. On the morning of Saint Patrick's Day, Ginny and Paul showed up at Chris's apartment with a bottle of Harvey's Bristol Cream for their annual hat-making ritual. Chris was still in bed. The draperies were closed, he had not showered in days, and the apartment had the gloomy, purgatorial stench emitted by the deeply depressed. After rousing Chris, he sat at the kitchen table in his too-short bathrobe, the sight of him scaring Ginny to death and embarrassing Paul.

"Look what Mommy brought!" Ginny said, waving the bottle of Harvey's.

"Not for me," Chris replied. "Go have a good time."

"Not without you," Paul said. He'd never known Chris to turn down a drink.

"No way," Ginny chimed. But Chris would not be budged. After several awkward minutes of sitting with him in the kitchen, and not knowing what else to do, Paul and Ginny left Chris's apartment feeling like terrible friends.

The posse called an emergency meeting. Myrna, Lucy, Frank, and Pearl listened to Ginny and Paul's report. There was no doubt that Chris was in trouble and slowly killing himself. They all agreed there was no guarantee that, at this rate, their beloved buddy would still be with them in five years. Myrna, Lucy, Ginny, and Pearl agreed that something had to be done. Frank and Paul were on the fence. Paul said, "I'm not my brother's keeper. It's his life, if he wants to eat himself to death."

Frank agreed with Paul. Pearl accused Frank of being cold. She was tired of her husband's aloofness. Emotions made Frank uncomfortable. At the first hint of confrontation, introspection, discussing feelings, advice-giving, Frank was likely to run for the hills. Pearl did not like Frank's passivity, believing that friends deserved more hands-on treatment. It was far too easy, she thought, to allow those you loved to sink without lending a hand, to walk away from friends in need, to avert one's eyes, and not to get involved. The world was full of people who did this, and Pearl believed it was wrong. In Pearl's opinion, her husband, Frank, and Paul represented much of what was wrong with the live-and-let-live society: disinterest masquerading as respect for boundaries; self-absorption when people needed a life raft. "We need to be his life raft," said Pearl. "We cannot let him drown."

"It's none of our business," Frank said.

"When someone you love is killing himself, it becomes your business," Pearl replied sharply.

"We can't just sit here and do nothing," Lucy agreed. "He's been there for us. We should be there for him."

"One hundred percent," Myrna said.

"But how?" Ginny asked.

"We'll find a way," Pearl promised. The men were not so sure but decided to keep their doubts to themselves.

Three thousand miles away, at a Pilates studio in West Hollywood, Louise and Polly were considering their own potential intervention with a friend in trouble. Amanda, their third musketeer, was dating a man who appeared to be some kind of gangster. Parker was an Irish immigrant with no visible means of support and a talent for finding merchandise that fell off trucks. One week, it was refrigerators (fifteen of them), which Parker was selling for cash only. Another week, Parker was selling name-brand computers for next to nothing. Then it was lawn mowers. After that, it was satellite dishes. Certainly, Parker's lifestyle was extravagant for an undocumented alien without a job. Parker owned a triplex apartment on the beach, enjoyed courtside season tickets for NBA games, and wore a large gold skull ring on his right wedding finger. Parker also had a smashed-up nose job that looked as if it had been operated on with a baseball bat.

Amanda fell head over heels for Parker. He was the first man who'd shown any interest since her bitter divorce two years before. Like a high school girl with a teenage crush, she told Polly and Louise about meeting Parker in line at the car wash. They stood side by side watching their cars creep through the magic steam tunnel. Parker complimented Amanda on her Prius; he had a BMW hybrid that happened to be teal, Amanda's favorite color. They chatted about fuel efficiency and Al Gore, and, by the time their cars were ready to roll, Parker had asked for Amanda's phone number.

After they had been dating for two months, Amanda felt as if she were reborn, but Polly and Louise were apprehensive. Strange things had happened with Parker on several occasions. Once, Parker left Amanda at a restaurant before the entrée was even served, claiming that a friend needed help. Another time, he swerved off the freeway after a heated cell phone call and drove Amanda home without warning. When Louise researched Parker's name online, she found no trace of the pop band he claimed to have sung with in Dublin, the Muggers. Parker admitted to Amanda that he had an "unconventional" job with a group of fellow Irishmen but assured her that it was legit. This was worrisome enough, but when Amanda told her friends that Parker had invited her on a Hawaiian cruise, they panicked, imagining their friend disappearing at sea.

Louise was on the Pilates machine, her arms and legs splayed like a butterfly pinned to a corkboard. "Maybe we're wrong about him," she said.

"And maybe we're not," Polly answered, stretching on a mat.

"I hate to rain on her parade," Louise said.

"It's better than her funeral."

Both sets of friends, Chris's and Amanda's, found themselves at the fuzzy threshold where a friend's business does become our business because they are threatened with physical harm. We are ethically obliged to intervene in such situations, despite the chance of risking offense. We are called on to help because it is right. However inconvenient, frightening, or embarrassing, the first loyalty must be our friend's survival. Intervention is often difficult. We avoid addressing the truth when it may bring conflict. We agree to look the other way rather than face confrontation.

For example, I know a woman who smokes too much pot. She blames her dependency on rheumatoid arthritis and procures the pot from a legal cannabis dispensary. She believes that her doctor's note and dispensary card immunize her against being a plain old pothead. This would not be her friends' business were she not an emphysemic, paranoid shut-in, but she is. Still, there's nothing that we can do. Whenever someone mentions quitting—or cutting down—she banishes us from her house. This leaves the people who care about her in a state of suspended concern, frustration, and low-level dread. We can't take the pot away from her. And we can't pretend it's not doing her harm. We realize there's nothing that we can do to change her. But neither can we not be concerned.

Chris's friends couldn't stop caring either. Their buddy had lost his way, and they needed to do what they could to help him— whether or not the intervention was successful. They decided to plan a trip to Maine, where Ginny's grandmother had a house on a lake, without telling Chris. The six of them swarmed his apartment the morning they left and nearly dragged him out of bed. Outnumbered, Chris reluctantly agreed to come with them on the condition that he could come home if he wanted to.

At the lake house, Chris found a spot under a tree and sat there looking miserable while the others swam. After a while, he fell asleep on a blanket and remained there for most of the afternoon. His friends left him alone, watching Chris from the window, waiting for him to wake up. Finally, Chris rolled over and pulled himself to his feet. Instead of walking to the house, he wandered down to the lake while his friends watched through the window. Chris took his time lumbering toward the water, then sat on a bench near the boathouse where the loons used to build their nest.

After a while, Chris's six friends walked out to where he was sitting and found that he was crying silently, intensely, into his shirt. Ginny brushed a blade of grass off his chin and sat down on the bench beside him. Myrna took a place on the other side and put her arm around his shoulders. Chris just cried and cried. By the time they left five days later, Chris seemed to be feeling a little better. His gloom appeared to be shifting; by the last day, he was wading up to his knees in the cold lake. Chris's depression was not gone, but it had thinned up a bit. Glimpses of the old Chris were peeking through, rays of humor, moments of brightness. His friends began to believe that he was going to be alright.

Polly and Louise were less successful when they cornered Amanda. She was looking like a million bucks, better than Amanda had in years, thrilled that the cruise was a week away. Louise was the first to speak. "There's something we have to tell you," she said.

"There is no Muggers band in Dublin," said Polly.

Amanda shrugged. "So what?"

"Parker might not be who he says he is," Louise said. "We're scared that you might be in danger."

Louise's ominous tone made Amanda laugh. "In danger of what? Too much love? He's like a big puppy dog. He wouldn't hurt a flea."

"If something happened to you, we would never forgive ourselves," Louise said. When she tried to touch her friend's hand, Amanda pulled back. She felt as if they were conspiring against her. Suddenly, it occurred to her that she was always the third wheel here, the designated screwup, the one to be helped. In fact, there were only two musketeers and one who was always on probation. Amanda was tired of being judged. She was ready to have her life back. Amanda had met a wonderful man and had no intention of leaving him. She'd be on that boat to Honolulu whether Polly and Louise liked it or not, and when she returned, Amanda was not entirely sure that the three of them would still be friends. She would always know that they didn't trust Parker. She would know that they didn't trust her, either, to have an intelligent head on her shoulders. Amanda would know that when she needed to jump, these friends of hers had tried to stop her, whether or not it worked out with Parker. When she needed courage, they blocked her way. That was how Amanda saw it, blinded by her infatuation.

Polly and Louise only meant well, of course. Still, there was nothing that they could do but step aside and hope for the best. It was, after all, Amanda's life.

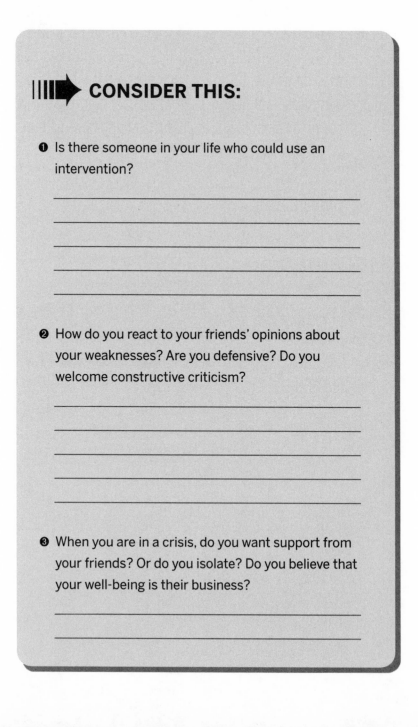

CONSIDER THIS:

❶ Is there someone in your life who could use an intervention?

_____

_____

_____

_____

_____

❷ How do you react to your friends' opinions about your weaknesses? Are you defensive? Do you welcome constructive criticism?

_____

_____

_____

_____

_____

❸ When you are in a crisis, do you want support from your friends? Or do you isolate? Do you believe that your well-being is their business?

_____

_____

❹ Have you ever turned away from a friend who needed your help and regretted it afterward? What would you have done differently? Why?

TWENTY

Long-Distance Friends

B romance can catch a straight man off guard. That is what happened with Gregg and Mike. They met during a year abroad as visiting professors at Florida State University's campus in Florence, Italy. Both men were single, good-looking, intellectually ambitious, and enjoyed sports. On the weekends, they drove up to Fiesole, on the hill above the city, and played racquetball at a club where both were members. Afterward, in the late afternoon, with the red roofs of Florence spread out before them, they drank Campari and soda and thanked God that they weren't in Tallahassee, swatting mosquitoes and fighting boredom on the home campus.

If Gregg or Mark had been a woman, they would have been in love. As it was they looked for women together, played a lot of hot-and-heavy racquetball, ate unforgettable meals, took an overnight train down to Calabria—the sole of Italy's boot—on a whim, and revealed a greater depth and breadth of intimacy than either young man had ever enjoyed with a woman. Gregg and Mark were surprised by this unexpectedly close friendship but had no qualms since both were heterosexual. As the end of their abroad year approached, they enjoyed the last months of Tuscan splendor and worried together over drinks in the Piazzale Michelangelo about how they'd survive back home next year. The thought was unpleasant to both of them, but at least they'd be in it together, they agreed, like soldiers going back to war.

Three weeks before semester's end, a phone call came from the department chairman, offering an extended year for one of them, not both. This was an emotional bombshell. Another year in Florence was impossible to turn down, but which one of them should get it? And what about their new bromance? Mark and Gregg did the only sensible thing they could do: they tossed a coin and it went to Mark to fly back to that hellhole near the Gulf three weeks later.

Left behind in his favorite city, Gregg felt unexpectedly blue. The winning ticket felt empty and cold in his hands. Their favorite haunts—the sports club, the gelateria, even the strip joint—felt as sad as a room where the party has ended. Mark, on the other hand, was oddly relieved to be home. He was happy to sleep in his own bed, and he even called Trish, the ex-girlfriend he'd been thinking about. Mark thought about Gregg, of course, and missed their conversations, but found himself having easier, deeper talks with Trish than they had the first time around. He'd been practicing the art of personal connection with Gregg. Mark now found himself using a voice with Trish he did not know he had. Trish fell back in love with the Mark she always hoped was there underneath the mask, and Mark responded in kind to her warmth. As Mark's relationship with Trish got more serious, he thought less and less about Gregg, who, in turn, felt him slipping away.

Long-distance friendship is like a tug o' war. One friend withdraws, the other advances, back and forth in the push and pull of displaced people struggling to hold onto a bond that has no place in their daily lives. Gregg was aware, painfully, of Mark's withdrawal and tried connecting on Skype every weekend. At first, this was awkward, waving to each other through their computer screens, but Gregg and Mark soon settled into their easy groove. Gregg "met" Trish on Skype, always a surreal experience, attempting to "know" a pixilated image beamed across the planet, but he did his best not to show his disgust as Trish nuzzled Mark's neck, filling Gregg with a new kind of jealousy. He restrained himself from faux-vomiting (one of his and Mark's favorite laugh gags) when Trish kissed Mark's cheek and thanked Gregg for sending him back from "It-ly" in one piece. Trish was an "Amurrican" through and through, and her hickishness, along with her proximity to Mark, drove Gregg up the wall.

As the weeks went by, Gregg's mood worsened. Why on earth was he feeling so bereft? His sadness made him think about his mother, who had died eight years before of cancer. Why was he thinking about her now? It didn't make any rational sense. And why was this missing his mother connected to how he was now missing Mark? Gregg's mind was in a tangle as he walked along the cobblestone streets.

One Sunday afternoon, his loneliness was so unbearable that he sent Mark a postcard—Gregg had never sent a postcard before in his life—with grains of rice actually glued on the card from their favorite risotto place. Missing Mark made him philosophical. What did it mean to know someone long distance? How could you feel deeply bonded with someone while tolerating masses of missed information, the gaps and silences, the sense of being off their radar screen? How could you feel both attached and unattached, loyal yet undemanding? Mulling over this, Gregg began to wonder whether love itself, all human relationships, carried an impossible riddle at their center about how big you had to be, how generous, to really love another person, and how he was always falling short.

For the first time in his life, Gregg experienced the fact that it actually *hurts* not being able to share the details of life with the people you care for. Gregg felt nostalgia for the small details of their friendship. He had never realized the preciousness of small things in friendship or how precise longing for a long-distance friend can be. You don't want to talk to just anyone. You want to talk to *this* friend, because only this particular person knows you in this particular way and gives you a sense of being home.

Strangely, this pining for Mark's friendship, the depth of feeling it opened in him, made Gregg a more interesting person. He was callow, arrogant, and shallow before. He scoffed at others' inability to overcome their emotions—especially women—because he could not feel his own. Being proudly rational, Gregg had missed out on half his experience. Now, he was seeing the world in a different way, as if someone had pounded on his chest, leaving him a little sore all the time. This ache made him see the world with more compassion. "I've been there," a voice inside his head muttered when Gregg passed a woman in the street who was crying, instead of muttering, "Stifle it, wench." He felt softer, that was the word for it, which was strange, new, a little scary, and irresistible to women. He also felt more compassion for Trish, who was not so heinous after all. She was simply unschooled. Gregg realized that unless he connected with Trish, he was dooming his friendship with Mark, especially with geography against them.

There's a saying about emotions and alcohol: The more you drink, the more yourself you become, the more truthful, for better or worse. *In vino veritas*. The same principle holds for long-distance friendship. The farther friends live from one another, the more their friendship will show itself for what it really is— or isn't. When Gregg and Mark were separated, what arose (for Gregg especially) was longing, followed by self-understanding, followed by expansion and tolerance for the sake of the friendship. This accentuation of their affection was a testament to the health of Gregg and Mark's friendship bond. The same could not be said of Vanessa and Anna.

Anna liked Vanessa more than Vanessa liked Anna. Through-out their eight-year friendship, Anna secretly suspected this. But when Anna moved into her apartment complex, shortly after they met, Vanessa's indifference had been able to ride undetected on a daily stream of sheer convenience. This changed when Vanessa's husband was offered a new job a thousand miles away. Vanessa felt liberated from Anna's cloying, porcelain presence, the sense that if you blew on her too hard she would crack. Anna was the sort of woman who used her own delicacy to dominate others (the way sick people sometimes use their illness to get their way), but this tactic didn't work long distance. Vanessa could not avoid Anna in their common hallway but could certainly postpone, indefinitely, responding to Anna's plaintive voice mails. Anna was crushed by Vanessa's indifference and told her so when she finally got her on the phone.

"Are you avoiding me?" Anna asked.

Vanessa said, "Nope."

"If you want to cut me off, just tell me so." This was another of Anna's maneuvers: accuse the friend of wanting out. Go to the worst scenario. She was used to Vanessa backpedaling but now, on the phone, this did not happen. Vanessa did not dignify Anna's stupid statement with a response. She'd had enough. With geography on her side, Vanessa had her power back.

Anna shrank into instant submission. "I'm sorry. I'm so sorry," Anna said. Vanessa tuned her out. She knew the drill. Anna now would put herself down so badly that Vanessa would be expected to say, "Oh, no, you're wonderful." But Vanessa didn't do this either. When Anna's self-butchery was over, Vanessa said nothing.

Anna dangled there like a plucked chicken turning in the wind. She did not know what to say and hung up the phone, fuming. She was angry at Vanessa and wanted to hurt her. But what could she do from another city? Anna suddenly recognized that she had no hold on Vanessa whatever; and what did that say about their friendship? To Anna, friendship centered on control—all relationships to Anna were about control. You knew that you were connected to someone by the degree of control they had over you or vice versa. Anna did not know the difference between control and caring. Vanessa would be tyrannized no longer by Anna's woes. Safely long distance, she could finally be honest. Long distance required that Anna and Vanessa mend their friendship or let it go.

The first rule of long-distance friendship is: regularity based on shared commitment. I learned this from my friend Adam. We've been close friends for twenty years although Adam and I have not shared a city since 1998. Still, he is indefatigable about not slipping a millimeter in emotional closeness. He achieves this by demanding face time—one of us visiting the other's city—and regular phone time if I know what's good for me. This isn't as needy as it sounds: Adam simply makes no bones about whom he loves and his unshakable, regular need to see them. Care draws care. He is also among the most beloved people I know. Adam stays friends with people all over the world, maintaining intimate connections, in spite of physical separation.

The second rule of long-distance friendship is: thou must cut slack. Adam believes that friends are in one another's lives to make those lives easier, not more complicated, and that we must be flexible and cut slack when life interferes. Communication becomes more difficult long distance; sometimes planning a phone call with a friend in Australia is like orchestrating a peace conference. It's hard but necessary being patient with friends' efforts, and important not to hold them hostage to grudges over last-minute changes.

Gregg and Mark have been working on this one for the past few months, ever since Gregg met Melinda and canceled two Sunday Skype sessions in a row, because he and Melinda were skiing in the Alps. Mark's cheeks burned when he got the second texted cancellation. He and Trish were frying in the Tallahassee heat, and not getting along as well as before, and the thought of Gregg and Melinda—the hot waitress from their risotto place— slaloming on powder in Switzerland made him want to punch something. He missed Gregg like crazy and noticed how missing him made him sad, which was the last thing that Mark wanted, and how his sadness made him turn on Trish. Mark had never before noticed how feelings spill into one another with obvious but inevitable imprecision. Seeing this, Mark felt closer to Trish. Missing Gregg made Mark a deeper person. The bromance helped him learn to love.

CONSIDER THIS:

❶ Have you ever lost a friendship due to long distance? If so, what happened?

_____

_____

_____

_____

_____

❷ Have you noticed the connection between longing and love? Do you find longing painful?

_____

_____

_____

_____

❸ Is it hard for you to reveal love for friends? To show them how much you care, when they are far away?

_____

_____

_____

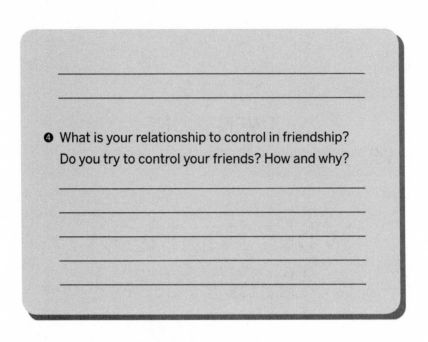

❹ What is your relationship to control in friendship?
Do you try to control your friends? How and why?

TWENTY-ONE

When Friends Are Brainwashed

I had never witnessed a friend being brainwashed until Carlo met Reverend Matt Gerrigan. Carlo, a dear friend from childhood, had always been impressionable. The first in our circle of friends to discover mood rings, holotropic breathwork, crystal aura cleansing, colonics, and the Tao of Tennis, Carlo was a diehard seeker. He investigated past-life regression, gestalt therapy, and a special brand of Amazonian footwear guaranteed to replenish positive ions lost by the feet in the act of walking. We respected Carlo's determination to stretch his suburban envelope—to attain spiritual enlightenment, even—but regretted his gullibility. Carlo's ability to convince himself of almost anything, until the next big thing came along, was remarkable and dangerous.

When we lived together in San Francisco, the next big wow was Reverend Matt, a self-proclaimed healer and speaker in tongues who held forth from a moveable pulpit every Sunday somewhere in the vicinity of Haight-Ashbury. Carlo became a regular at Reverend Matt's ludicrous Christian-esque meetings. Wearing a Hawaiian shirt unbuttoned to the waist, and blathering on about suffering, disease, and financial struggle being no more than illusions we could rid ourselves of through positive thinking, Reverend Matt was the kind of snake-oil charmer you used to see outside circus tents, selling magical elixirs, promising eternal life if you promised to give him a lot of money.

Carlo was intoxicated by Reverend Matt's message, which promised eternal liberation for the price of membership to his church. He dragged me to one of Reverend Matt's meetings, where I sat, aghast at his tacky theatrics and the shallowness of his sunny message, while the Reverend's helpers passed the hat and he soaked the unquestioning, unfortunate souls who'd wandered into his congregation. Many of his followers appeared to be desperate characters, sick people on their last legs, poor people hoping to get rich, outcasts hoping for a place at God's table, which Reverend Matt claimed to promise them as long as they were obedient. I watched helplessly as Carlo fell under this charlatan's spell, outraged by this quasi-religious nonsense and the ripping off of people in genuine need.

But Carlo would not be reasoned with. Spiritual charlatans are dangerous precisely because they prey on people at their most vulnerable opening, the part in us that wants God or longs for connection to something transcendent. Our brains are wired for religious experience whether we believe in a God or not, and spiritual jingoes like Reverend Matt are the moral scum of the ethical earth for exploiting this need with fakery. Being gullible, credulous, and willfully innocent, Carlo leapfrogged logic and reason straight into the lap of this holy fool, leaving his friends stunned and worried.

Rape has many forms, and brainwashing is one of them. To see a person brainwashed is to see them violated. Their unawareness that this is happening, or their desire to appear unaware, makes the rape even worse. Five of us—three friends from college and Carlo's soon-to-be ex-girlfriend, Heidi—sat Carlo down at a restaurant for an intervention. Carlo knew exactly what we were doing and was ready with Reverend Matt's defense.

"He loves people," Carlo said. "He helps them. I witness this. He is beyond duality."

"What the hell does that even mean?" asked Heidi. "Listen to yourself."

Carlo smiled that fake beatific smile meant to cover the fact that he was very pissed off and cocked his head at Heidi, who cocked hers back, sarcastically. I asked Carlo if he believed that we loved him. He gave a reluctant yes. I asked if he thought that his five best friends were stupid. "Obviously not," he replied.

"So when we tell you that you are being fleeced by an obvious fake and turning into someone we don't recognize, shouldn't that be a smidgen of cause for speculation on your part?" I suggested. My anger at Reverend Matt made me testy.

Our questions left no dent in his certitude. After the useless intervention, Carlo hugged each one of us, giving that same fake smile, and told us he would pray "on" us. Reverend Matt was always getting them to pray *on* something. The following Sunday, and every week after that for a year, Carlo continued going to Reverend Matt's church with increasingly alarming results. The reverend counseled his flock to become macrobiotic, which took twenty-five pounds off Carlo's already lanky frame and made him look a prison-camp worker. He had quit his job at an accounting firm and now worked half price for Reverend Matt's operation. Carlo's friends watched helplessly as he withdrew to this strange magnetic, parallel world with its own customs, language, moral code, and expectations circling a charismatic leader. It was crazy, sad, and infuriating. Carlo has never been the same in my opinion, though Reverend Matt is long gone, having left the state to avoid prosecution for tax evasion.

Religious brainwashing is one thing; recovery brainwashing is something else. Then you have political brainwashing, romantic brainwashing, and countless other types of brainwashing. The effect of all brainwashing is the same, though: to replace our individual mind-sets with dogma in the process of making us loyal to a party line, the voice box of an ideology, a follower whose personal parts have been covered over to turn us into Stepford wives. Some ideologies are better than others. It is better to be brainwashed by Suze Orman than it is to be brainwashed by the KKK. But even positive brainwashing has the effect of replacing individual thought with an "ism" of some kind or other. (Suze Orman-ism, for instance, is frugal but rigid, practical but bossy around the edges.)

Ideologies appeal to us because humans like authority, giving control over to "higher powers," and being submissive to individuals who seem to know more than we do. Ideologies hook us because we can become part of something larger than our small selves ("I'm in the Tea Party" sounds more formidable than "I'm an unemployed pipe layer with anger issues"). We can follow their lead and coast down a beaten, well-traveled path. As group dwellers, there is great comfort in being able to say, "I am [fill in the blank], and we believe this [fill in the blank]." The heavy lifting of figuring things out is done for us (by Reverend Matt, or bad therapy, or vegans, or Feminist.com), which gives us the illusion of safety, belonging, and self-assurance. Following authority figures also frees us to be undiscriminating, to accept things we disagree with, and be manipulated into behavior we would avoid if we were in our right mind. Brainwashing resists debate, compromise, and exploration; it deflects insight and helps us become entrenched in erroneous thinking. It can also cause defensiveness and a sense of threat when outside views are expressed without regard to the party line.

I had such an experience when speaking to a friend in a twelve-step program. The "Twelve Steps" are wonderful, powerful, life-changing tools, among the most effective brainwashing programs we have invented in this country, but they do not encourage personal choice. My friend had been sober for twenty years and worshipped the Twelve Steps, which she credited with saving her life. Out of idle curiosity, I asked her if she could imagine a time when she'd no longer need to attend meetings. My friend snapped, all of a sudden, angrily accusing me of not really "getting [her] journey." That would be code for not knowing who she really was. I assured her that I knew who she was and was, simply, curious to know how the meeting commitment evolved over time. Asking this question had been a big no-no; for a while, she didn't trust me. Ironically, this friend of mine no longer attends meetings and wouldn't consider taking a drink. This was the possibility I had been wondering about.

Romantic brainwashing is ubiquitous in a culture that worships romantic love. Like all ideologies, romantic love has its iron-clad code of ethics, its terminology, its own peculiar illogic, and its own esthetic. To say that something is romantic is to suggest a particular flavor of experience, a standard, a level of emotional beauty, or unusual display of affection. When our friends fall in love, we lose part of them to the demonic god Eros, part of them to the pleasure god Dionysus, and the rest of them to insecurity. They see the world through a romantically brainwashed lens that's impossible to clear with logic. When Karen said she was going back with LZ, her friends wanted to throttle her. But when LZ called, Karen always followed, brainwashed by dopamine, estrogen, and the seductive moves of a two-faced man.

Here is how the cycle worked: Karen, who'd broken up with

LZ at least five times that I knew about, for reasons that had not changed, would try again to dump him, stay away for a month or two, then succumb to loneliness and the brainwashing story she had told herself for most of her life: Women who live alone are losers. As an extrovert, Karen did not enjoy solitude. She was also a diehard romantic who defined her life through men, what arc of the romantic journey she was on, where she was in the process of loving, and how much closer she was to her goal of marriage and kids. LZ was the only man with whom she might have wanted children; he was the only man who knew she liked peonies, and Arby's roast beef, and was phobic of bats when LZ got her to go camping. He was inseparable from the romantic story that gave Karen's life meaning. Although Karen did not know it, she, like all brainwashed people, had been inhabited by a meme.

Memes are ideas that replicate virally in populations, as I described in *Ethical Wisdom*. From the Greek for "something imitated," memes range from beliefs to melodies, catchphrases, fashions, fads, and ideologies that are spread through the behaviors that they generate. Memes range from innocuous slogans ("blonds have more fun") to hate speech ("Jews killed Jesus") to calls for benevolence ("save the planet by living 'green'"). The Internet has ramped up memetic imitation by a factor of millions, as networks like Twitter and YouTube spread images and ideas instantaneously around the clock and around the globe.

Brainwashing occurs through the memetic process. We are exposed to a meme that takes root in us, and our lives become manifestations of those beliefs. We're unaware of how easily brainwashing happens and how we can guard against it. Many people fail to question their own thoughts. Out of laziness, conformity, fear, or lack of patience, we do not take the time to examine the contents of our own minds, leaving them easy marks for random memes to control us in unexamined ways.

Take Karen, for example. Ordinarily a bright, curious, accomplished woman, she "dumbed down" whenever she went back with LZ; she lost a piece of her own perspicacity. Brainwashed, she became voluntarily stupid, unable to use her own mind to save her. Hijacked by emotion, Karen's romantically addicted mind led her wherever it wanted while she went limp, driving her friends completely crazy. They knew what would happen— that LZ would cheat—and they knew how harsh Karen's landing would be when she crashed, yet again, on the same concrete floor. They knew that they would have to help pick up the pieces because they loved Karen and would not desert her. But her inability, or unwillingness, to wake up and smell the mofo kept her in a cycle of loss and longing.

The one thing Karen could not do was question her own beliefs. She could not attain the necessary distance, or give credence to the rational voice in her head. Hijacked by feeling, the voice of reason turned to static, removing Karen from the seat of personal power. In order to gain distance from our own thoughts, many excellent mindfulness techniques exist. Journaling and meditation are both highly effective as mirrors to our inner world. "Until we question our own thoughts, we suffer," spiritual teacher Byron Katie reminds us. This may sound obvious but, upon reflection, that single bit of advice could save a lot of people millions of dollars in therapy bills (though I have nothing against psychotherapy) by testing it on their own lives.

That is exactly what happened with Karen. Unlike Carlo's intervention, which ended with no separation from the brainwasher, Karen's friends had better luck when she kicked LZ out the last time, and Karen hit the skids. Unlike Carlo, Karen was tired of suffering and open to her friends' suggestions. They told her it seemed as if she had been brainwashed, and maybe she needed to question—the story, the meme—and find out what was propelling her out of control again and again. Karen looked puzzled when they used the word "brainwashed"; then she looked interested. Even in our craziest moments, the wisdom-mind exists behind the tumult; the truth is waiting behind the lie. Karen's eyes registered some kind of recognition of the notion that her mind had actually been taken from her. It became, for her, a first step to deprogramming and the bridge back to herself.

CONSIDER THIS:

❶ How have you been brainwashed in your life? What specific ideologies have formed your worldview?

_____

_____

_____

_____

_____

❷ Have you ever questioned a belief and been able to let it go? How did you do this?

_____

_____

_____

_____

_____

❸ What memes affect you in your daily life? Are there memes that are destructive that you would like to be free of?

_____

_____

_____

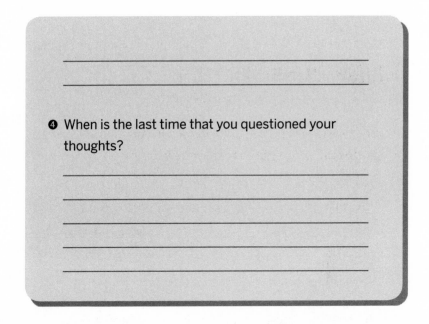

❹ When is the last time that you questioned your thoughts?

TWENTY-TWO

The Party Animal

College had ended ten years before, but Jason never got the memo. At thirty-two, wearing his caveman hair, surfer shorts, multiple earrings, and cartoon tattoos, Jason resembled your average hard-drinking, bong-toting party-animal freshman. But those days were ancient history. His signature puckishness—skateboarding everywhere, ogling hot chicks, being hung-over (or looking it)—eccentricities that once seemed semicool, now were just embarrassing and sad for a married sanitation worker with twin daughters attending Montessori school in the suburbs of Ann Arbor, Michigan.

Jason didn't want to grow up. On the day of the incident, the T-shirt he was wearing had the AARP logo on the back and I'D RATHER BE DEAD across the front. When Jason and his wife, Amber, arrived at Heather and Max's condo, Jason was in normal party-hearty, wasted-again-in-Margaritaville mode. His unwashed hair was dusted with glitter from last night's concert, his breath a stinking furnace of booze that made Heather wish, instantly, that she had not poured mimosas. As brunch ensued, Heather could not miss the exhausted expression on Amber's face as she watched Jason throw back his third mimosa. Heather wished her long-suffering friend would divorce this Peter Pan lush of a husband, but she knew also that if she asked how things were, Amber would claim to be content and reject the idea that anything was wrong.

By his fourth mimosa, Jason was flying, a blur of sweaty belly flesh in the backyard Doughboy pool, where he was splashing around with Sam, Heather and Max's three-year-old, balancing the boy in one arm and his drink in the other hand. One of the downsides of Jason's drinking was its effect on his ability to hear. With each cocktail, Jason would become increasingly deaf to what people around him were trying to say. By the time he was hammered, he was impossible to communicate with in any kind of adult way. Knowing this, Heather had sent her husband to keep an eye on Jason and Sam, but now Max seemed to be half hammered himself in his lawn chair, not paying much attention to anything. When Jason accidentally dropped Sam on the asphalt, splat, with blood everywhere, in the process of draining his glass, Max could not move fast enough to catch him. Jason wasn't sure what happened, at first; then he focused on Sam face-down on the ground, ripped the side of the pool climbing out of the Doughboy, and looked confused as Max lifted up his bawling son and slammed the back door in Jason's face.

The scene went from bad to worse. Furious and ready to fight, Max handed off Sam to his mother and began hurling a litany of pent-up disgust at Jason, accumulated over many years. He went on and on about Jason's arrested development, his refusal to grow up, his desperate, embarrassing, last-ditch attempts to hold onto the last strands of his wild youth. Amber and Heather watched helplessly as Max ripped into his old friend, saying terrible, unforgiveable things, till Amber finally intervened, and walked shell-shocked Jason to the car, apologizing again to Heather and looking like she wanted to die. When Max locked the door behind them, he told Heather this was the last time that bozo was setting foot in their house.

Excess has its place in moderate doses. But excess can only be enjoyed to the degree that we have mastered it. Otherwise, the lush becomes the alcoholic, and the bon vivant turns into the pig, and the naughty friend declines into someone whose mis-chief makes our life worse not better. This can be a slippery slope between friends. Most of us don't like playing the scold. An inte-gral part of close friendship is the ability to let your hair down, indulge in the extra glass of wine, stay up too late, be bad. Being bad together is good for friendship. You don't know a friend till you've seen them hammered—or they are in recovery.

Good ethics include vice and disorder, a touch of chaos, the ability to be Dionysian—drunk, inappropriate, who-the-hell-cares—now and then under controlled conditions. As important as Apollonian traits of constraint, reason, and conformity are, so are the Dionysian impulses of freedom and fun. "Dionysus's dominion includes all states of being that entail loss of self-awareness and rationality, the suspension of linear time, and the abandonment of the self to those urges in human nature that overthrow codes of behavior and public responsibility," to quote psychologist Philip Zimbardo once again.

But how do we deal with excessive friends in a way that respects them and protects us? Friends who are out of control are not our biological allies (people whose company makes us feel better) but are our biological enemies, pressuring us to overindulge and join their magic-carpet ride. I used to know a writer like that. This fellow was brilliant, the life of the party, a walking laugh riot. But the party never stopped. He lacked any speed but fifth gear; every night was an opportunity to get more wasted than the night before. This writer brought with him a "pharmacy of bliss," which always included alcohol and sometimes Schedule II narcotics. Everyone loved him, which didn't help. That's the tragedy of friends like this; the people around them turn them into characters and write them off. This writer careened off the map and died suddenly from a hemorrhage of the esophagus. He was only forty-four. In bars and taverns around town, so-called friends ordered rounds in his honor and remembered his brilliant mind, pickled in decades of gin and tequila.

It's toxic trying to have too much fun. When friends are excessive, we may feel compelled to follow them down Satan's highway. This is important to admit. If we convince ourselves that we're invulnerable, and immune to peer pressure, we let down our guard and deceive ourselves. Situational pressure, and changes in hormone levels, can lay our moderate impulses to waste. In one study, people in their twenties were asked five questions about their propensity to engage in "questionable activities," such as unsafe sex. Their predictions, made in a cold, rational state, were off by more than double (136 percent) compared to when they were aroused. In a set of questions about using condoms, these teens were 25 percent more likely to predict they would forgo condoms in the aroused state than in the cold state. They largely failed to predict the influence of arousal on their morality and approach to safe sex. Prevention, protection, conservatism, and moderation were tossed aside in a hormonal hurry.

Combine our tendency to overestimate self-control with the bad influence of excessive friends and you get a recipe for destruction. When friendships are polluted by overindulgence, their foundation is weakened. When one or the other friend cleans up his act, the other friend may get left behind. This happened to Louise and Roberta. This pair of thirtysomething singles watched too many episodes of *Sex and the City*, using their biweekly happy-hour dates to get too happy, too often, with too many unforeseen consequences. Once, they ended up in a rapper's van being offered lines of cocaine off a CD cover. That was the wake-up call for Louise, who had more self-control than Roberta, her partying friend who had no brakes. The next time they got together, Louise, on the pretext of taking antibiotics, drank only ginger ale and watched as Roberta got plastered and wound up shimmying alone on the dance floor while people giggled and stared. Louise saw her future if she didn't change. After that, she never called Roberta for reasons she was too embarrassed to mention. This was a shame since Roberta might have learned something.

As for Jason, he made a crash landing. Max stopped speaking to him, and Heather could only see Amber alone. Feeling ashamed, and painfully dropped, Jason stewed in remorse for most of a year. While stuck in this depressive rut, he watched a lot of TV, switched from hard liquor to beer, played more with his daughters, and found himself working extra hours at the office, which got him a promotion and a bit of self-esteem. One day, Jason saw Max across the gym and took a chance, walking over to him. At first, Max didn't recognize him. Jason had cut off his hair and removed his earrings. By the time Max realized who he was, Jason had given him a hug.

"You look good!" said Max, happy to see him.

"I'm sorry," said Jason.

"I know you are."

That was the extent of the conversation. But it was enough to heal their wound. Max was glad to have this Jason back in his life. He didn't miss the other guy.

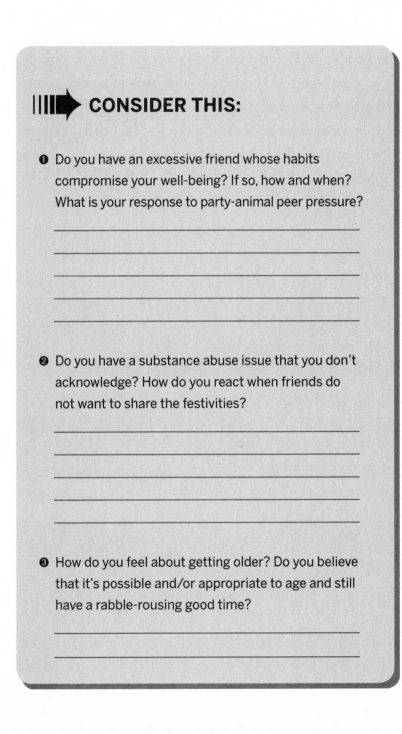

CONSIDER THIS:

❶ Do you have an excessive friend whose habits compromise your well-being? If so, how and when? What is your response to party-animal peer pressure?

_____

_____

_____

_____

_____

❷ Do you have a substance abuse issue that you don't acknowledge? How do you react when friends do not want to share the festivities?

_____

_____

_____

_____

_____

❸ How do you feel about getting older? Do you believe that it's possible and/or appropriate to age and still have a rabble-rousing good time?

_____

_____

❹ Have you ever ended a friendship because the friend
was overindulgent? What happened? Did you talk to
your friend about your objections?

TWENTY-THREE

Friends Who Don't Listen

When Steve moved to Seattle, he had no friends. As a thirty-eight-year-old schoolteacher, newly separated from his wife, Steve left his familiar life behind in Indianapolis and was anxious to meet new people—women, of course, but also some buddies—to ease his transition from jilted husband to not-yet-middle-aged, not-bad-looking bachelor, footloose and fancy free in the Pacific Northwest.

Jerry seemed like the perfect candidate to become Steve's new friend. A fellow tennis player and family physician, Jerry chatted

up Steve in the steam room one day and the two began playing tennis on alternate Saturdays. Jerry was happily married, with
four kids, but relished the time away from his brood to whack
a ball around with a buddy. Steve welcomed the company and
believed, for the first couple of months, that Jerry might become
a friend. Like Steve, Jerry had a sarcastic sense of humor, voted
libertarian, and liked to loiter in sports bars. After their Saturday
match, the two would repair to a bar in the neighborhood, drink
beer, watch football or baseball, and talk about absolutely nothing. Rather, Steve would talk about nothing while Jerry rambled
on about work, family, and the price of gas, anything that crossed
his mind, while Steve listened, grateful to have a friend to hang
out with on lonely Saturdays in this strange new place where
nobody knew him and it rained cats and dogs.

A few months into their friendship, Steve got a call from his
wife, Rhea, asking for a divorce. Steve was devastated. He'd har-
bored a secret hope that time apart would heal them, but Rhea
had fallen in love with someone else and was ready to move on
with her life. That Saturday, Steve arrived at the club feeling devastated, but Jerry didn't seem to notice. They played a couple
of lousy matches, Jerry insulted Steve's backhand, and Steve
attempted to keep his mind on a tennis ball bouncing around a
court. Jerry creamed him game after game. Afterward, the two
men sat in the steam room and listened to naked men in towels
talk about elbows, shin splints, and hockey, then made their way
to the sports bar. Steve needed to talk, badly, and assumed that
Jerry would want to listen.

Focused on the baseball game and mozzarella sticks, Jerry did not seem to register Steve's mood, which made Steve feel even worse. "I'm having a hell of a week," he told Jerry.

Jerry's eyes were glued to the TV screen. "If the Mets don't get their act together—"

"Rhea wants a divorce," said Steve.

Jerry glanced at him, said "Good riddance to bad rubbish," and slapped Steve on the back. "How about we order some wings? These friggin' cheese things are always cold."

"I can't believe she met somebody else so soon."

"Jay-sus!" Jerry yelled at the screen. "You believe these guys? Pay attention!" Steve stopped trying to talk. An angry sadness rose up in him. He felt like he did when he was a boy, trying to talk to parents who never listened, either. All through a difficult adolescence (Steve had been a stutterer and painfully shy), he had needed to talk to them—his father especially—but could not seem to get their attention, leaving Steve with the sense of being uncared for, invisible, mute, and unacknowledged. Rhea tuned him out the same way; in truth, Steve had no one in his life who seemed to know how to listen. It wasn't that Steve had nothing to say (although Rhea accused him of being boring); instead, he seemed to attract people who shared an attention deficit. Jerry was simply the latest person to turn a deaf ear when Steve was talking. But why did he magnetize these people, Steven wondered later that day, alone in his soundless apartment? Was it something about *him* that failed to command attention? Were his speaking skills so pathetic, he wondered, or was Rhea right and he was boring? When Steve got nervous, he could fall into stuttering, still, after all those years of correction. Perhaps people sensed him trying too hard and it embarrassed them? Or maybe Steve only chose nonlisteners because he was used to being ignored?

In a soulful book called *My Grandfather's Blessings*, Dr. Rachel Naomi Remen writes about the lost art of listening, and why people like Steve feel so lonely even among so-called friends. Overwhelmed by media, gadgets, distractions, and alternative means of communication, we've forgotten that listening is a form of love, Remen writes, and that our stories—the narratives of our inner lives—are largely what bind us together. "Our lost art of [listening] and telling stories accounts for a cultural loss of soul and shared insight into how we live," she explains, pointing to the pre–e-mail tradition of people sitting around and talking. "Because we have stopped listening . . . we have stopped learning how to recognize meaning—and to fill ourselves—from the ordinary events of our lives. When we stop telling each other our stories, we seek out experts to tell us how to live." Friends seeking wisdom, comfort, and connection pay therapists to listen to them—as Steve was about to do—and forget what the simple act of listening can do for people in need of human reception.

We are storytelling animals. It is through storytelling that we survive. Language enables us to tolerate experience. Narrative helps us to manage disorder. Communication enables us to handle emotion by passing along our stories to others. "All sorrows can be borne if you put them into a story or tell a story about them," novelist Isak Dinesen reminds us. There's a beautiful story about an Israeli woman who'd gone to a therapist because she was having trouble breathing. As they spoke, the therapist noticed the camp numbers tattooed on the patient's forearm. The woman coughed a great deal while telling her story.

"When did you start having trouble breathing?" the therapist asked.

"When my friend died two years ago," the survivor admitted. "When she was alive, we could talk about anything. Although she wasn't in the camps, she understood. But now there is no one to tell. And the nightmares haunt me. I can't sleep alone in the house. I know that if I want to live, I have to find another friend."

That is why the act of confession is considered a sacrament. Witnessing another confess is a holy act. In our listening (as well as our telling), we remind one another that we are connected on this human journey. A good friend knows this. A good friend knows that when we are in pain, the greatest gift they can offer is the chance for us to empty out our troubled minds into the attention of someone who cares. We rarely need to be told what to do; we never want to be lectured at; what we long for is a friend to hear us, and nod, and laugh, and remind us that we have been through crazy times before, and that it will pass. We will be okay.

I see this with students all the time. Teaching memoir writing, I'm privy to people's loneliness and the common refrain of people feeling unheard. Students tell me things they have not told their closest friends. Some secrets are romantic, others traumatic—one recent secret was criminal—but all attest to this same isolation. Phyllis was a case in point. At forty-five, with a shy personality and few friends, Phyllis lived alone in a rent-stabilized apartment near Boston without even a cat to talk to. She was one of the saddest people I'd ever met, profoundly sweet, extremely loyal, but unable to keep friends or lovers around. To compensate for her loneliness, Phyllis slept with every man who would have her and lost respect for herself in the process.

When Phyllis started to write her stories, and have them read by our class, her isolation started to shift. She seemed shocked that someone (even a paid teacher) would be interested in what she had to say. Revealing parts of herself that she was ashamed of, dreams she had not dared to admit, Phyllis poured out her trials and tribulations. She wrote heartbreaking stories about her childhood, screeds to her long-dead mother. A lifetime of grief surged up in Phyllis, but expressing it was not damaging. On the contrary, she seemed lighter and less burdened. I did little but listen to her stories and watched her change, beautifully, before my eyes from a quiet, distant, unhappy person to a woman full of experience and unexplored strength. The simple act of being listened to brought Phyllis back to life like magic. Now, she has moved on to an actual therapist who is doing her tremendous good.

Steve also found a therapist. A month went by without seeing Jerry, who'd been traveling on business. When they ran into each other at the club, Jerry did not ask Steve how he was. They played a couple of games of tennis and then found their regular stools at the sports bar. Jerry was his usual distracted self, but Steve, encouraged by his therapist, was unwilling to fade into the background. He mentioned that the divorce was proceeding and

Rhea was being worse than ever. "It was her idea and she's playing the victim."

"What are you going to do?" Jerry asked without listening. He flagged down the waitress for calamari and turned his attention to the TV.

"Have you always been this way?" asked Steve.

"What way?" Jerry replied.

"Unavailable," said Steve.

Jerry turned from the game and focused on him. "What is that supposed to mean?"

"You don't listen," Steve said.

"I sure as hell do!"

"No. You don't."

"Really?" Jerry asked. "That's what my wife always says."

"She's right," Steve replied. "It's not your best feature."

Jerry stared at him. "Maybe you're right," he said slowly, popping a squid strip into his mouth.

"You're a doctor."

"Sorry," said Jerry. "I guess I'm a jerk."

"You're not a jerk. You just need to listen."

"I'm sorry about the divorce," said Jerry.

Steve replied, "I appreciate that" and turned his attention to the ball game. The calamari disappeared. They didn't say very much more that day. It was no longer necessary.

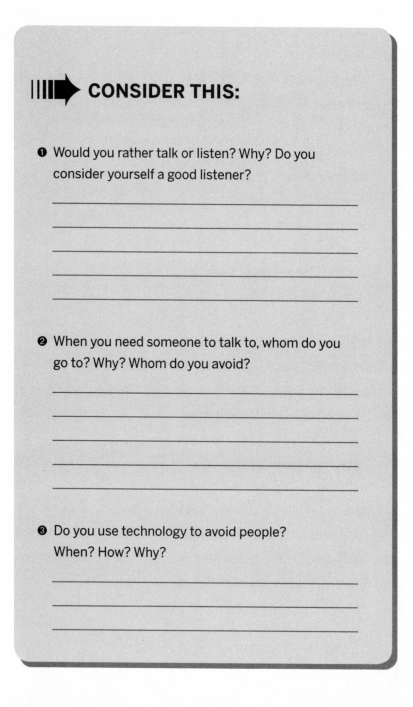

IIII➤ CONSIDER THIS:

❶ Would you rather talk or listen? Why? Do you consider yourself a good listener?

_____

_____

_____

_____

_____

❷ When you need someone to talk to, whom do you go to? Why? Whom do you avoid?

_____

_____

_____

_____

_____

❸ Do you use technology to avoid people? When? How? Why?

_____

_____

_____

_____

_____

❹ Describe an experience of needing to confess a
secret or a painful experience. What did you learn?

_____

_____

_____

_____

_____

TWENTY-FOUR

Breaking Up

The upside of life's most difficult experiment is that it always comes with a wisdom lesson, an insight you might never have had without first getting kicked in the teeth.

I learned this myself when those four friends dumped me over the incident involving gossip. Unfair as their rejection may have been, it also taught me something useful: namely, that people can *choose* to go their own way when a friendship isn't working for them. As a stick-around guy raised on the belief that hanging in is what matters most, come hell or high water, the notion of simply choosing to move on was completely novel to me. I remember the cavalier note that one of them sent me at the time. In it, she explained that, after long reflection, she simply needed to "close the door." Although this hurt it also came as a revelation. A person could choose to close the door? No drama or negotiation? Just like that? Really? Who knew?

This wisdom came in handy with a friend named Devon. Opportunistic, superficial, and distracted, Devon was lively company but hard to trust, his handsome nose always pressed to the ground, seeking connections and money trails like a hound sniffing for truffles. Devon wasn't a bad person, just predatory and shamelessly self-serving. I allowed our sort-of friendship to drag on for years . . . till one afternoon when Devon and I were having our umpteenth coffee date with him pumping me for freelance advice, and I realized I didn't need to do this again. The incessant careerist treasure hunting had worn me down. I'd had enough with the charade of friendship. The honest thing was to walk away. No meaningful conversation was necessary because our friendship wasn't meaningful (that was the problem). The next time that Devon called, I said I wasn't available. Unlike a true friend confronted by a stone wall, he never bothered trying to find out what was wrong. His glaring disinterest confirmed my suspicions, and the two of us went our separate ways.

Friendships are affairs of the heart, though we rarely think of them that way. Like all such affairs, they have their seasons, their autumns and springs, and sometimes they don't survive a long winter. Like all forms of love, they sway and dip, and must be allowed to change if the friendship is to weather life's transitions. Effie could never understand this. She hated ebbs and flows in friendship. Effie rejected change on principle because change equaled risk, and risk equaled loss, and loss threatened to leave Effie alone.

As an adopted child, Effie never knew her true identity, and this mystery left her feeling ungrounded. Her well-meaning but undemonstrative adoptive parents did nothing to relieve this rootlessness. Effie lived on a limb of abandonment ready to snap at any moment, and this gaping internal void made her an emotional vampire. She was clingy, needy, accusatory, and fully convinced that all of her friends were poised to leave her. This fear became a self-fulfilling prophecy; Effie drove people away with her paranoia. Still, she did not understand why this happened until one day in her therapist's, Martha's, office. Effie was forced to connect the dots.

"I hate change!" she said for the hundredth time.

"Hating change is hating life," said Martha.

"I don't hate life," Effie disagreed.

"Life is change," the therapist told her. "You can't like one without the other."

"Maybe I'm just too screwed up to have friends," Effie said, sinking down into her chair. She knew that Martha was right. But it was also true that she hated change. Change more or less spelled disaster. Change had delivered the baby Effie to parents who didn't deserve her after Effie's biological mother's life changed by getting pregnant. This was the tangle in Effie's mind: the essential mis-telling of her own story. Effie clung to her friends for security though it squeezed the life out of other people. In Effie's "creation story," Martha explained, change equaled abandonment. She would need to question her own beliefs, and slowly change this fearful behavior if she hoped to stop chasing people away. "You're not that abandoned baby anymore," Martha told Effie. "People are life. Change is life. People change. Do you get my meaning?"

"Not really," Effie said.

Unfortunately, at this precise moment, Effie's closest friend, Selene, was on the threshold of calling it quits. Effie and Selene had been vacation-away, holiday-together, type of friends for the past fifteen years. The problem was that Selene was married and had a family, while Effie was single and suffering from an attachment disorder. This meant that Effie always wanted more and Selene was always trying not to feel as if Effie was sucking her blood. Effie was just too high maintenance. The interminable phone calls (Effie was famously hard to get off the phone), the reassurances, the explanations, the re-explanations. Selene couldn't take it anymore. She made a date with Effie to break up—at least have a trial separation—but she was dreading it. She did not want Effie to hate her. But she also had no logical reason for thinking that this would not happen.

When Effie saw Selene, she noticed how stressed out Selene looked.

"Are you okay?" Effie asked.

"I'm okay," said Selene, noticing that Effie was looking rotten, too. Selene braced herself for Effie's barrage of her latest list of catastrophes, the horrible things people had done to her, the ways that others had let her down, never giving Effie a fair shake.

But strangely enough, this did not happen. Instead, inexplicably, Effie asked Selene question after question about how things were going with her, the crappy job, the family, work, even the anti-anxiety meds that Selene's doctor had prescribed when her blood pressure spiked. Martha had suggested to Effie that she experiment with asking her friends about themselves first, just to see what happened. Selene was taken off guard by Effie's attention and found herself unexpectedly enjoying her company. Midway through their breakup lunch, Selene realized that she had not done the breakup talk. The thought of not seeing Effie seemed suddenly less appealing. Too extreme. Too abrupt. The next time that Effie drove her crazy, Selene would be sure to talk to her. At least, that's what she told herself.

It's heartbreaking to lose a friendship. It is also sometimes necessary. Men tend to be less tortured about losing friends than women are. When male friendships break up, it is often done without verbal exchange; we withdraw, starve out, freeze out, deny, and obstruct intimacy, indirectly, like cowards. This is easier for men to do because our friendships themselves often lack deep emotional content. Male friendships, like Steve and Jerry's (in the previous chapter), tend to center around impersonal activities. When men break up as friends, the absence of communication is less conspicuous. Women, more emotional and demonstrative, are also more complicated in their breakups. Breaking up is often more difficult because they know one another better than male friends do.

Tabitha and Marge were like that, and their story ended nowhere as happily as Effie and Selene's. Tabitha annoyed the hell out of Marge. Marge complained about Tabitha behind her back and often wondered why she tolerated her frenemy's annoying habits (which included hoarding and stretching the truth). But Marge also knew Tabitha's troubles, and Tabitha knew Marge's all too well, and this empathic connection through pain held them together like a dark cord. Many of the qualities that Marge loathed in Tabitha were intolerably like aspects of herself. Marge needed to cut things off with Tabitha. Unfortunately, she did not know how.

Each time that Marge sidled up to the subject, her willpower sank like a hollow soufflé. Marge felt herself go all gooey inside, too sticky and sad and sentimental to broach the subject of ending their friendship. Tabitha was constantly in crisis, so there was never a good time (it's so much harder to dump someone when they've just been dumped). This kept Marge in a vortex of resentment and inaction. Where two men might have knuckle bumped and said so long—or walked away, like I did with Devon—Marge wrung her hands and waited, and waited, the permanent dislike of Tabitha clenched like a dark fist inside her belly.

What Marge didn't know was that Tabitha felt the same way about her. She didn't enjoy Marge's company. They were enmeshed, co-addicted, unhealthily bonded, and Tabitha knew, secretly, that she would not miss Marge at all after she figured out how to leave town. What did that make them, Tabitha wondered? Family? Ech. Friends? Not really. Companions? Now, that just turned Tabitha's stomach. Marge's "companion"? Tabitha would rather be institutionalized.

The climax came for these friends over an incident involving money, which was ironic since neither of them had any. Tabitha borrowed five hundred dollars from Marge to pay for her health insurance. Tabitha promised to repay the money within the month, which was prerequisite since Marge had borrowed it from someone else. The month came and went, but Tabitha made no moves to repay it. As the fourth week of dead silence wore on, Marge found herself in such a rage that she could neither eat nor sleep. When Tabitha sent the fateful postcard, therefore, the ground was already mined for explosion. Tabitha made the awful mistake of sending Marge a postcard from Florida, where she had gone unexpectedly with her ex-boyfriend, presumably on Marge's dime. Marge sat at her kitchen table and wrote Tabitha the meanest letter she'd ever written, forced herself to put it into a drawer, then bought a postcard of an old hag in rhinestone sunglasses and saggy boobs on Miami Beach, with a message that said, "Happy trails. Marge" and sent it to Tabitha. She could not continue with this woman. Tabitha had gone one step too far. The two of them never spoke again.

Breaking up with friends is more uncharted territory than breaking up with a lover or spouse. With friends, there are no rituals, precedents, or traditions for ending the relationship. We make little allowance for the fact that friendships *are* affairs of the heart; wrenching emotions draw little sympathy (it's not like you were *sleeping* with them). Friends are neither kin nor sexual partners so we're not supposed to feel deep grief over their loss. Forgetting that friendship is a form of intimacy, we make no provisions for heartbreak. But breakups between friends deserve the compassion and patience offered automatically to the romantically wounded. Reconciliation between friends is equally worthy of celebration and pride. Effie marveled to her therapist in the weeks after averting disaster with Selene that she was finally learning to be a good friend. She was learning about her friends in a whole new way. Instead of feeling like they owed her something, she was concentrating on asking more questions, showing them that she cared and was actually worth keeping. Effie was learning to resist the urge to use guilt as a way of getting attention and even agreed to Selene's suggestion that they have a "safe word" on the phone that would allow Selene to hang up regardless of what Effie was carrying on about. This compromise alone was enough for Selene, who felt that she was at last being heard in their friendship. Effie was doing her best not to complain as much or rely upon sympathy as a way of medicating her insecurity. There were better ways to bond with people, she realized, ways involving give-and-take, and having a lot more fun.

||||➡ **CONSIDER THIS:**

❶ Whom do you want to break up with in your life?
How long has this been going on?

_____

_____

_____

_____

_____

❷ How do you respond to anger and confrontation
in friendship?

_____

_____

_____

_____

_____

❸ Do you think of friendship as an affair of the heart?
Why? Why not?

_____

_____

_____

❹ Do you believe that friendship is forever?
Or that friends are wise to move on when things
get tough together, because there are so many
fish in the sea?

About the Author

Mark Matousek is the author of two award-winning memoirs, *Sex Death Enlightenment: A True Story* (an international bestseller) and *The Boy Be Left Behind: A Man's Search for His Lost Father* (Los Angeles Times Discovery Book), as well as *When You're Falling, Dive: Lessons in the Art of Living*. A featured blogger for *Psychology Today* (where his Ethical Wisdom column appears weekly) and the *Huffington Post*, he has contributed to numerous publications including the *New Yorker*, *O: The Oprah Magazine* (where he was contributing editor), the *New York Times Magazine*, *Harper's Bazaar*, *Yoga Journal*, the *Chicago Tribune*, *Details*, *AARP*, *Tricycle: The Buddhist Review* (contributing editor), and many others. A popular lecturer and writing teacher, he is creative director of V-Men (with Eve Ensler), an organization devoted to ending violence against women and girls. His latest book is *Ethical Wisdom: The Search for a Moral Life*. Learn more at www.markmatousek.com.